HAPPY TRAILS

YOUR
COMPLETE GUIDE
TO FUN AND SAFE
TRAIL RIDING

HAPPY TRAILS

Les Sellnow

**ECLIPSE
PRESS**

Lexington, Kentucky

Library of Congress Control Number: 2004104475

ISBN 1-58150-114-5

Printed in the United States
First Edition: October 2004

Distributed to the trade by
National Book Network
4720-A Boston Way, Lanham, MD 20706
1.800.462.6420

A Division of
Blood-Horse Publications
Publishers Since 1916

Contents

EQUINE BREEDS
Something for Everyone

Horses of all breeds can make suitable trail mounts. Through the years I've worked with and ridden horses representing most of the breeds discussed in this chapter. I've found good ones and bad ones in every breed.

When it comes to choosing an appropriate trail horse, select a mount that fits your personality, level of horsemanship, and riding style. Beyond those three basics the choice is wide open. Unless you're already committed to a particular breed, my advice is to shop and test-drive as many breeds as you can.

You'll find most breeds have inherently unique characteristics (both physical and psychological) that make selecting a new horse somewhat less complicated. Look at these traits as you would the sticker sheet on a new car — as a guide to what you're getting. But just as you would test drive any new car, don't rely on the sticker for all the information you need. Look at the individual horse because there are exceptions to every rule.

Exceptions to the Rule

If you were to generalize, it would be safe to say that Arabian horses excel at long-distance riding. Year in and year out, more Arabians finish in the top ten of the prestigious and grueling one hundred-mile Tevis Cup than any other breed. And logically so since the breed developed in the deserts of Arabia, where it had to travel great distances in hot, dry weather with little food, water, or rest.

Another generalization might be that stock horses, such as Quarter Horses, Paints, and Appaloosas, are the best equipped for climbing and descending steep mountain trails because of their powerful hindquarters, developed over generations of ranch work.

Then there are the gaited breeds, such as Missouri Fox Trotters, Tennessee Walking Horses, and Pasos, developed for their smooth gaits and comfortable ride. While they might not have the endurance of the Arabian or the power of the stock horses, they can cover ground, even rugged terrain, faster than other breeds. Yet, there are always exceptions to these general rules. There are Fox Trotters and Walkers that are as powerful as Quarter Horses. There are Arabians that don't possess great endurance and Appaloosas and Pasos that certainly do.

Grade horses, which are non-registered horses with varied backgrounds, also make fine trail mounts. These horses are not registered with any breed organization and often their ancestry is unknown. However, remember that every grade horse descends from some breed; and if you examine the horse's conformation and type, you'll have a clue as to which breed or breeds might be its ancestors. Knowing the breed of origin can help you guestimate the horse's potential for success as a trail-riding mount.

Breed prejudice aside, I think it's important when you are selecting a trail horse to know something of its background and breed characteristics. But in the end, it all boils down to finding the horse that pleases you.

Here's a rundown of the major breeds, listed alphabetically, and some general information regarding their history, temperament, and characteristics.

Appaloosa

Native Americans in the Northwest, who took great pride in their horses, developed the Appaloosa, producing a hunting and war horse with speed and stamina, as well as an amenable disposition.

However, horses with Appaloosa spots on their coats did not develop in North America. Based on depictions in ancient art, spotted horses are as old as recorded history. The Spaniards brought them to the Americas during their years of conquest, beginning in the 1500s. But the horse's history actually goes back some 20,000 years, with renditions of what is now known as the Appaloosa appearing in drawings on cave walls in France. Later horses portrayed on Chinese and other Asian artifacts clearly depicted the Appaloosa coat pattern.

After the Spaniards brought them to this country, horses with Appaloosa coloring eventually fell into the hands of Native Americans, who, by the 1730s, were mounted on these exceptional animals. The Nez Perce and the Palouse tribes of Washington, Oregon, and Idaho were the first Native Americans to conduct a selective breeding program, and using the Appaloosa they produced strong, athletic horses. The name Appaloosa is thought to derive from "a Palousey," a term that white settlers in the Northwest

The Appaloosa is known for its distinctive coloring.

Territory called the spotted horses they saw. The name, taken from the Palouse River or the Palouse tribe, was eventually changed to its existing form, Appaloosa.

The number of Appaloosas reached its pinnacle with the Nez Perce tribe in the 1870s. Shortly thereafter, the breed nearly met its demise because of the war between the Nez Perce and the U.S. cavalry. The tribal leader, Chief Joseph, traveling with women and children as well as warriors, led the cavalry on a months-long chase through 1,300 miles of rugged mountain terrain.

The Nez Perce and their Appaloosas met a sad ending when Chief Joseph was forced to surrender just shy of the Canadian border toward which he and his followers were fleeing.

Almost overnight the once proud and undefeated breed was in danger of disappearing. The cavalry, in essence, declared the Nez Perce Appaloosas to be machines of war. They were taken from the Indians and either destroyed or scattered; many of the stallions were gelded. Concerned horsemen soon began gathering the Appaloosas that remained, launched breeding programs, and in 1938 formed the Appaloosa Horse Club.

While the Appaloosa is a breed in its own right, it also may contain genes from other breeds. Prior to the formation of the registry, some of the early breeding programs were aimed at maintaining the Appaloosa color pattern rather than a particular breed standard.

Modern breeding programs have changed that approach, and the Appaloosa of today is a versatile animal that can be an excellent trail horse. But, as with all breeds you look at for trail riding, it's best to check on the individual horse's temperament by taking a close look at its pedigree. Find a family line that has a reputation for producing calm, tractable horses with sound conformation, and you might find yourself a trail horse that not only is a pleasure to ride but has a colorful coat as well.

And don't forget stamina. Remember, these are the horses that kept ahead of a well-mounted army with the luxury of replacing mounts as they wore out. A well-conformed Appaloosa trail horse should stay sound even over rough terrain and have the stamina to go all day without becoming exhausted.

In addition to a colorful coat Appaloosas have other physical characteristics that set them apart: striped hooves, mottled skin, and sclera around the eye. Appaloosas must be at least fourteen hands tall to be registered, and they may range up to sixteen hands or more.

For more information: Appaloosa Horse Club, 2720 W. Pullman Road, Moscow, ID 83843. Phone: 208-882-5578. Fax: 208-882-8150. E-mail: aphc@appaloosa.com. Web: www.appaloosa.com.

Arabian

The Arabian is considered the oldest purebred in the world, and many of today's light horse breeds, such as the Thoroughbred and Morgan, descend in part from the Arabian. The Bedouin tribes of Arabia may not have domesticated the horse, but they are the first horse owners to carry out breeding programs. Through many centuries they bred the best to the best, putting proven stallions to proven mares in their bands. Owning a band of horses with good conformation and endurance enhanced the standing of any Bedouin chief or warrior.

The goal of those early breeders was to produce a horse that would satisfy their needs. The desert is not overflowing with vegetation, so the horse had to be thrifty. It was also a long way between water holes, so the horse had to have endurance.

The Bedouin lifestyle often involved raids on enemy camps. The tribal warriors traveled to the point of attack on camels, while leading the war horses, and after the raid

The Arabian has stamina.

sped across the desert on their sturdy little steeds to escape angry pursuers.

Thus, the Bedouin needed a horse that could sustain itself on little food and water and still have both speed and endurance. Large horses just didn't fill the bill, so the Bedouin developed a small breed that had good bones, tendons, and muscles; great lung capacity; and a willingness to travel miles without slacking.

Generally, Arabians are 14 to 15.1 hands and weigh between eight hundred and a thousand pounds. The typical Arabian has a beautiful head, with generous width between the eyes, tapering down through a dished face to a fine muzzle.

Anatomically, Arabians are different from other breeds in that they possess one less vertebra in the back and one or two fewer in the tail. Traditionally, they travel with plumed tail and proud head carriage.

As a trail horse, an Arabian can be excellent — depending on temperament. Perhaps the best trail horse I ever owned was a gray Arabian gelding. He had a calm, gentle temperament and would go anywhere I asked, provided it was safe. If he refused to set foot in a particular area, I knew in a heartbeat that it was dangerous. I've also ridden Arabians that were high-strung and fidgety, jumping and prancing at any movement along the trail.

If an Arabian or half-Arabian is your horse of choice, then learn all you can about the horse's breeding. If it comes from stock that's high-strung, with no trail-riding background, pass it by. If you're not knowledgeable about Arabian pedigrees, find someone who is. He or she should be able to tell you, for example, that a particular bloodline is noted for show-ring charisma but is so high-strung that it would make a poor choice for a trail mount. Your expert should also be able to recognize pedigrees that are populated by solid riding horses with calm temperaments.

But remember, there are exceptions to every rule. A horse is an individual, even if its bloodline is not noted for producing trail horses. The best indicator is observation. Pay close attention to the horse's temperament. Does it seem fidgety and nervous, jumping at every sudden movement, or is it calm and quiet? Obviously, you are looking for the calm, quiet representative of the breed.

Arabians' stamina also stands them in good stead on the trail. They'll often be full of energy at the end of a long day when other horses are drooping.

For more information: Arabian Horse Association, 10805 Bethany Drive, Aurora, CO 80014. Phone: 303-696-4500. Fax: 303-696-4599. E-mail: info@arabianhorses.org. Web: www.arabianhorses.org.

Missouri Fox Trotter

The Missouri Fox Trotting Horse developed in the rugged Ozark hills in the nineteenth century. Missouri achieved statehood in 1821, and the pioneers who poured across the Mississippi River and settled in the Ozarks came largely from Tennessee, Kentucky, and Virginia. They brought with them horses that had been popular in those areas, including Saddlebreds and Tennessee Walking Horses, along with a mixture of Arabian, Morgan, Standardbred, and plantation horses. The settlers found horses that could travel with the easy, broken gait called the fox trot were useful in the rocky, forest-covered hills of the Ozarks. Before long they were breeding large numbers of horses for this unique gait.

When traveling at the fox trot, the horse walks with the front feet and trots with the hind feet. This sure-footed gait gives the rider little jar since the hind feet literally slide into place. The fox trot is a rhythmic gait, and the horse can maintain it for long periods with little fatigue. The Missouri Fox Trotter also performs a rapid flat-foot walk and a canter.

Before the advent of paved roads and cars, Missouri Fox Trotters were the breed of choice for cattlemen, sheriffs, doctors, tax assessors, and business people. Today the breed is still used extensively on ranches in the Ozarks but also has become the trail-riding horse of choice for many people because of its comfortable gait and normally gentle disposition.

In 1948 in Ava, Missouri, fifteen people concerned with preserving the breed founded the Missouri Fox Trotting Horse Breed and registered a number of horses in the Douglas County area. However, the organization suffered a setback when fire destroyed the studbooks and records along with the secretary's home.

In 1958 the breed reorganized and today is one of the fastest growing of the gaited-breed associations.

For more information: The Missouri Fox Trotting Horse Breed Association, P.O. Box 1027, Ava, MO 65608. Phone: 417-683-2468. Fax: 417-683-6144. E-mail: foxtrot@goin.net. Web: www.mfthba.com.

Morgan

The Morgan is the only breed that traces its lineage to one horse: a stallion named Figure, owned by Justin Morgan, a Vermont teacher, composer, businessman, and horseman.

Figure was foaled in 1789. Although his actual breeding is still open to debate, some people believe he was of Thoroughbred and possibly Arabian descent because his sire is listed as True Briton, a horse said to be "of the best English blood." Others argue that the cross was actually Arabian and Friesian, and maybe even some Welsh Cob.

The Morgan is versatile.

Figure was a dark bay with a refined head and compact body. For short distances he could outrun most horses put against him. He was also a fast trotter. In addition, he could out-pull horses that outweighed him by a couple hundred pounds or more.

The breed has changed

some through the years. The short, stocky look of the old-style Morgan has given way to horses with a bit more leg and refinement, partly due to the show-ring environment and the preferences of show-horse breeders. Some horsemen have criticized that today's show Morgan looks more like the Saddlebred than the traditional Morgan.

Morgans, however, still are powerfully built horses ranging from about 14.2 to 16 hands. Their sturdy bodies can carry heavy loads, and they have the stamina to endure for hours on end. They're extremely versatile and can make excellent trail-riding mounts. Generally speaking, they have quiet temperaments and excellent hooves. But pick your trail horse carefully. You don't want a show-ring peacock — you're looking for a solid trail companion. The best endurance horse I ever competed on was half-Morgan and half-Arabian.

For more information: American Morgan Horse Association, Box 960, Shelburne, VT 05482-0960. Phone: 802-985-4944. Fax: 802-985-8897. E-mail: info@morganhorse.com. Web: www.morganhorse.com.

Paso Fino

Paso Finos are known for their smooth, ground-covering gait. In fact, the breed's name means "the horse with the fine step." Paso Finos have existed in Latin America since the days of the conquistadors but were virtually unknown in the United States until the late 1940s.

The Paso Fino is a mixture of three breeds — Andalusian, Barb, and the now extinct Spanish Jennet, from which it most likely inherited its four-beat, lateral gait.

It's believed that Columbus, on his second voyage to the New World, transported this breed's ancestors to what is now the Dominican Republic, where they were used to replenish the remount stations of the conquistadors. Over hundreds of years their popularity spread throughout South America and Central America.

Paso Finos are not large horses, varying between 13.2 and 15.2

hands, with the average being slightly over 14 hands. They have refined heads; arched necks; sloping shoulders and croups; and long, flowing manes and tails. Their hooves are extremely durable. Many owners don't bother shoeing their horses unless traveling in rocky terrain.

While the Paso Fino can walk and canter like its equine counterparts, its preferred way of going is its own natural four-beat gait. Footfall is in the same sequence as an equine walk — left rear, left fore, right rear, right fore. The Paso Fino gait is performed at three forward speeds and with varying degrees of collection.

The gait most often used on a typical trail ride is the Paso Corto. It's performed at moderate speed — comparable to a trot on the average trail horse — ground covering but not excessively fast. A well-conditioned Paso Fino can travel at this gait for hours on end without tiring. At the same time the ride is smooth as glass for the rider.

With their smooth, ground-covering gaits and gentle nature, Paso Finos can make outstanding trail companions. However, as with other show-oriented breeds, select your mount from stock noted for performance on the trail and not show-ring presence.

For more information: Paso Fino Horse Association, 101 N. Collins Street, Plant City, FL 33563-3311. Phone: 813-719-7777. Fax: 813-719-7872. Web: www.pfha.org.

Peruvian Paso

The Peruvian Paso is touted as the breed that can guarantee its natural gait 100 percent of the time. Because for centuries Peruvian horses were bred only to each other, foals from the mating of purebred Peruvian Pasos will always inherit the breed's four-beat lateral gait.

Just like with Paso Finos, Spanish conquistadors introduced ancestors of Peruvian Pasos to the New World. The invaders brought with them horses of Andalusian, Barb, Friesian, and Spanish Jennet blood. These horses spread throughout the land, eventually arriving in Peru where breeders took great pride in mating the best to produce smooth-riding mounts.

When Peruvian Pasos travel, their front legs arch high and reach far forward, where they roll to the outside in a spectacular movement called *termino* — similar to the arm motion of a swimmer. Peruvian Pasos are the only horses in the world blessed with this showy action, and no artificial devices of any kind are needed to produce it. In fact, in horse shows in Peru and the United States, Peruvians are shown without shoes to emphasize the breed's natural action.

Peruvian breeders are also credited with developing the breed's excellent temperament by purposely not breeding animals with questionable dispositions. What horsemen got was a tractable and agreeable horse with great style, carriage, and *brio* (inner pride).

A typical Peruvian Paso stands between fourteen and fifteen hands, weighs about nine hundred to a thousand pounds, and comes in all solid colors as well as in gray and roan. The head is small and either straight or slightly convex in profile, the neck is short and arched, the body is deep and muscular, the mane and tail are luxurious, and the legs and hooves are strong.

Peruvians make excellent trail mounts and are often in competitive trail rides, where their good sense, gentle disposition, naturally smooth gait, and stamina are prized. But, as with Paso Finos and other finely bred show horses, make sure your trail partner is more interested in covering ground than in showing off.

Two associations serve the Peruvian Paso in the United States.

For more information: American Association of Owners and Breeders of Peruvian Paso Horses, P.O. Box 476, Wilton, CA 95693. Phone: 916-687-6232. Fax: 916-687-6237. E-mail: mjbpaso@msn.com. Web: www. aaobph.org.

Peruvian Paso Horse Registry of North America, 3077 Wiljan Court, Suite A, Santa Rosa, CA 95407-5702. Phone: 707-579-4394. Fax: 707-579-1038. E-mail: info@pphrna.org. Web: www.pphrna.org.

Quarter Horse

The American Quarter Horse has become the most popular breed in the United States, and some might argue, in the world. This versatile breed traces its origins to the 1600s, along the East Coast of the United States. The Quarter Horse is the product of the melding of various breeds brought to this country first by Spanish explorers and then by the English colonists. The Spaniards' tough mounts evolved into the West's premier cow ponies, and the settlers' horses were the famed racehorses that ran short-distance, one-on-one match races. Because the typical distance was a quarter of a mile, the fastest "Quarter Pathers" were called Celebrated American Quarter Running Horses. Most of them were heavily muscled and compact.

Sprinting speed in a large number of these athletes traces to a Thoroughbred named Janus, foaled in England in 1746.

In addition to the bursts of incredible speed at short distances, the

The popular Quarter Horse.

muscular, compact conformation of these horses also enhanced agility, especially when Eastern racehorses were crossed with Western cow ponies. When the great cattle drives took place northward from Texas in the 1800s, the horse that was to become the Quarter Horse added to its reputation as a versatile riding animal and outstanding cow horse. In the heyday of the huge ranches that followed in the wake of cattle drives, this type of horse continued to shine. It could cover ground during cattle gathers as well as use its strength and agility in roping and sorting.

In 1940 a group of ranchers met in Fort Worth, Texas, and formed what today is the American Quarter Horse Association. The AQHA is the world's largest equine breed registry, with more than four million Quarter Horses registered worldwide, and a recreational organization with more than 300,000 members.

There are many types of Quarter Horses. The ones used for racing and jumping generally carry more Thoroughbred blood and tend to be taller and rangier than their counterparts used for cutting or roping.

Quarter Horses are used extensively as recreational trail-riding animals. Normally, they are docile, strong, and durable.

Here again temperament and type are important. The odds of developing a good trail horse are better if you pick your Quarter Horse from stock known to be gentle and versatile, rather than from more high-strung racing stock.

The traditional Quarter Horse — one with a minimum of Thoroughbred blood — is an extremely powerful trail horse. Strong muscles in the rear quarters can power it up the steepest of trails, and those same muscles can be used as braking mechanisms when descending.

For more information: American Quarter Horse Association, P.O. Box 200, Amarillo, TX 79168. Phone: 806-376-4811. Fax: 806-349-6403. E-Mail: aqhamail@aqha.org. Web: www.aqha.com.

Saddlebred

The American Saddlebred is known as the peacock of the show ring. The breed conjures up images of a horse with nostrils flared in excitement, eyes opened wide, small ears pricked forward, traveling around an arena with a high-stepping gait; the rider, dressed in proper English show attire, either posting the trot or sitting the flying rack. That's an accurate image, but there's more to an American Saddlebred than flashiness. This breed results from America's melting pot of horses, and many Saddlebreds excel as trail mounts.

The chief progenitor was a horse named Gaines' Denmark, foaled in 1851 and the son of a Thoroughbred named Denmark, who excelled in four-mile races. The birthplace for the breed as such was Kentucky. Breeders in that commonwealth combined the blood of English riding horses with that of the Canadian Pacer, Narragansett Pacer, Morgan, Thoroughbred, and Standardbred. The blood of the Narragansett Pacer is believed to enable the American Saddlebred to travel at an ambling gait, called the slow gait when performed at a leisurely pace and the rack when performed at speed.

In a short time Saddlebreds spread throughout the South, and when the Civil War was fought in the 1860s, these horses carried the southern cavalry to war. The exploits of some of these horses are legendary, but there's a dark side, as is always the case in times of war. Many fine Saddlebreds were killed in battle, sometimes wiping out entire family lines.

When the war ended, there was a brief hiatus in the breed's development, and then it took off and now is spread across the United

The Saddlebred is comfortable to ride.

States, though the greater numbers remain east of the Mississippi.

If you want a Saddlebred as your trail horse, be sure to look for it in the right places. Do not go to a show stable and buy a horse that's seen nothing but the show ring for most of its life. Many of these horses spend their lives in box stalls to protect expensively shod feet and tailsets. This is not to say that a retired show horse or one that didn't quite make the grade can't be a good trail horse. Not at all; but the odds aren't in your favor.

Find a breeder who specializes in raising Saddlebreds for all-around use, such as trail riding and ranch work. Again, check family lines for temperament and, of course, check the horse itself for good conformation. In the sport of competitive trail riding, one of the winningest horses of all time is Wing Tempo, an American Saddlebred.

Saddlebreds, as a rule, are tall horses, with most ranging fifteen hands and up. Normally, they weigh between a thousand and twelve-hundred pounds. They have long legs to cover a lot of ground at the walk and are comfortable to ride.

For more information: American Saddlebred Horse Association, 4093 Iron Works Pike, Lexington, KY 40511-8434. Phone: 859-259-2742. Fax: 859-259-1628. E-mail: saddlebred@asha.net. Web: www.asha.net.

Standardbred

When we think of the Standardbred, we generally think of an animal that trots or paces while pulling a sulky around a racetrack. While many Standardbreds are involved in racing, this doesn't mean that they can't make good trail horses. Many Standardbreds are strong trail horses with solid hooves and great endurance.

The main progenitor of the breed was Messenger, a gray Thoroughbred imported to the United States in 1789. Of his descendants, a great-grandson had the most impact on the breed. The horse was Hambletonian, foaled in 1849. A poor farmhand, William Rysdyk, purchased Hambletonian as a foal, along with his dam, for $125.

Hambletonian never raced, but he was used as a sire from age two until his death at twenty-seven. It's estimated that the once-poor farmhand earned approximately half a million dollars in breeding fees during the horse's lifetime.

The name Standardbred was applied to the breed because from 1879 to 1933, eligibility for registration was based on the ability of the animal to trot the mile in the standard time of 2:30 or to pace it in 2:25. Today the fastest in the breed can cover a mile in less than two minutes.

Because of the animal's many fine qualities, Standardbred blood has been fused into other breeds, such as the Saddlebred, Tennessee Walking Horses, and other gaited breeds, during their developmental years. A Standardbred with sound legs is a horse that remains sound even in the roughest of country. Its durability is also a plus for trail riders. Again, be sure that the horse has a quiet disposition.

For more information: U.S. Trotting Association, 750 Michigan Ave., Columbus, OH 43215-1191. Phone: 614-224-2291. Fax: 614-224-4575. E-mail: sep@ustrotting.com. Web: www.ustrotting.com.

Tennessee Walking Horse

The Tennessee Walking Horse evolved out of agricultural necessity. The farmers of Tennessee wanted an effective utility horse that was also a smooth-gaited mount. They crossed lines of the Thoroughbred, Standardbred, Morgan, Narragansett Pacer, and Saddlebred, which eventually resulted in the Tennessee Walking Horse as we know it today. Some authorities even speculate that early Walking Horse breeders brought up gaited Spanish mustangs from Texas to cross on their pacing and trotting horses, thus introducing the four-beat, four-cornered gait for which the breed is famous.

In 1935 admirers and breeders of these horses met to form the Tennessee Walking Horse Breeders' Association of America. The organization selected 115 animals as foundation stock. Allan F-1, a small black stallion with a blaze face, was chosen as the number one foundation sire. He passed to his offspring a gentle temperament and a smooth running walk.

The Tennessee Walking Horse stud book was closed in 1947, meaning that beginning in 1948, to be registered as a Tennessee Walking Horse, both parents had to be registered.

Walking Horses are well known in the show ring, but they also make excellent trail mounts, as they are docile and sure-footed. They generally range in size from fifteen to seventeen hands and weigh an average of one thousand pounds.

The Tennessee Walking Horse has three basic gaits — the flat-foot walk, running walk, and canter. The flat walk and the unique running walk are both four-beat gaits, with each of the horse's hooves hitting the ground separately. The horse nods its head in rhythm with the gait, and its hind feet over-stride the tracks left by its front feet — left rear over left front, right rear over right front — sometimes by as much as eighteen inches.

In addition to its signature gait the Tennessee Walker can also perform the rack, stepping pace, fox trot, single-foot, and other variations of the running walk. While not acceptable in the show ring, these gaits are great for trail riding.

Again, proper selection is important. You'd do better to pick a trail mount from horses bred for that purpose rather from those bred and trained for the show ring. Tennessee Walking Horses are capable of carrying a trail rider for miles at a smooth, comfortable gait.

Tennessee Walking Horses come in all colors, including spotted. They have well-sloped shoulders and hips, short backs, and long underlines, giving them plenty of room for their long strides.

For more information: Tennessee Walking Horse Breeders' & Exhibitors' Association, P.O. Box 286, 250 N. Ellington Parkway, Lewisburg, TN 37091-0286. Phone: 931-359-1574. Fax: 931-359-7530. E-mail: twhbea@twhbea.com. Web: www.twhbea.com.

Thoroughbred

As is the case with the Standardbred, we generally think of the Thoroughbred in terms of racing. However, members of this breed are quite capable of being outstanding trail mounts. One of my top trail horses for several years was a Thoroughbred gelding with the very non-masculine name of Nangeline. He was well bred and showed great potential on the track at age three but then suffered a severely bowed tendon and was retired. He underwent surgery, recovered, and then served as a three-day event horse at the middle level of competition. He eventually landed in my hands and became an excellent trail horse. The only problem was that if a group moved off at a lope or canter, he became a handful unless he was leading the pack.

The term Thoroughbred describes a breed of horses referred to as "thoroughly bred." The animal's ancestry traces to three foundation sires — the Darley Arabian, the Godolphin Barb (some people say Arabian), and the Byerly Turk, named after their respective owners Thomas Darley, Lord Godolphin, and Captain Robert Byerly (also spelled Byerley). The stallions arrived in England from the Middle East around the turn of the seventeenth century and were bred to sturdy native mares.

This breeding program resulted in an animal that could carry weight at speed over extended distances. Needless to say, horses with this capability appealed to the many Englishmen who had a penchant for racing. That same enthusiasm carried over to America when horses of this type shipped to the New World.

In the early days of Thoroughbred breeding, records were sparse and frequently incomplete. In 1791 that changed when Englishman James Weatherby published the first volume of the *General Stud Book*, listing the pedigrees of 387 mares, each of which could be traced to one of three foundation sires: the famed stallion Eclipse, a direct descendent of the Darley Arabian; Matchem, a grandson of the Godolphin Arabian; and Herod, whose great-great grandsire was the Byerly Turk.

The first volume of the *American Stud Book* was published in 1873.

Because the Thoroughbred has been bred strictly for speed through many generations and not for conformation or temperament, trail riders should pay special attention to legs, feet, and disposition when deciding on the Thoroughbred as a trail mount.

A well-constructed Thoroughbred with a mild disposition can be a joy to ride. Such a horse has a lot of heart and doesn't know the meaning of quit. In addition, he can cover a lot of ground in a day of riding.

For more information: The Jockey Club, 821 Corporate Drive, Lexington, KY 40503-2794. Phone: 859-224-2700. Fax: 859-224-2710. E-mail: comments@jockeyclub.com. Web: www.jockeyclub.com.

Color Breeds

We look now at color breeds. Horses must demonstrate certain color characteristics before being eligible to be recorded by one of these registries.

Buckskin

The Buckskin is a very popular color breed and can be found on the trail in substantial numbers. The majority of buckskin horses are associated with stock horse breeds — Quarter Horse, Paint, and Appaloosa — but this coloring can be found in Morgans and in some gaited breeds, as well.

The buckskin color is ancient, often referred to as "primitive," as it afforded protective coloration to horses in the wild. It's said buckskins (or duns) have good, hard feet and lots of stamina.

In the American West, horses of the buckskin, dun, red dun, and grullo hues trace to the mustang — horses of Spanish Barb descent that originated in Spain as the Sorraia.

Other buckskins brought to this country can be traced to the Norwegian Dun, descendant of the nearly extinct Tarpan horse.

For more information: American Buckskin Registry Association, P.O. Box 3850, Redding, CA 96049-1420. Phone: 916-223-1420.

Or, the International Buckskin Horse Association, P.O. Box 268, Shelby, IN 46377. Phone/Fax: 219-552-1013. E-mail: ibha@netnit-co.net. Web: www.ibha.net.

Paint

Of the several color breeds that are popular as trail horses, perhaps the favorite today is the Paint, which has as its base the blood of Quarter Horses and Thoroughbreds. Paints are basically the same as Quarter Horses in conformation.

Spanish explorers brought horses with the Paint horse coloration to the New World. Later the animals found their way into the herds of the Native Americans, who prized them as great war horses and hunting horses. American Indians preferred the loud-colored mount to its solid-colored counterpart. Paint horses can be found depicted on buffalo robes or story skins, as the Indians called them.

There are two main color patterns for Paints — overo and tobiano. Overo horses generally have white under their bellies and on the sides of their abdomens and necks. The white usually does not cross the back of the horse, and the mane and tail normally are one color.

Tobianos have large, distinct, round patterns of white that extend

The Paint is a popular trail horse.

down the neck, back, withers, and chest, and the flanks are usually of a dark color. Manes and tails are often bi-colored.

A combination of tobiano and overo characteristics is called a tovero.

In 1962 admirers of these colorful horses decided to preserve both the color pattern and stock horse conformation that many of these animals exhibited. They formed the American Paint Stock Horse Association, which merged with the American Paint Quarter Horse Association in 1965 to become the American Paint Horse Association.

Today the APHA is one of the fastest growing and most progressive breed associations in the United States. Paints are sought after as all-around horses, especially performance horses, where they're popular in western pleasure, reining, and cutting. They also excel on the racetrack.

But where the Paint reigns supreme is as a family and recreational trail horse. Pick your Paint trail horse from colorful bloodlines, and you should have an attractive, eye-catching mount wherever you ride.

For more information: American Paint Horse Association, P.O. Box 961023, Fort Worth, TX 76161-0023. Phone: 817-834-2742. E-mail: askapha@apha.com. Web: www.apha.com.

Palomino

The Palomino is also a color breed. Horses with this distinctive golden or yellow hue can be of a variety of breeds, but there are key requirements for registration in the breed's main registry, the Palomino Horse Breeders of America. Horses should be from 14.1 to 17 hands. The mane and tail must be white, silver, or ivory with no more than 15 percent dark hair permitted. The eyes should be brown, black, or hazel. The body color should be near as possible to a newly minted gold coin, but various shades from light to dark are permitted.

Cortez introduced Palominos into America during the 1500s. There is evidence that these horses, originating from Barb stock, had long been bred for color in Spain and were used as mounts for royalty.

There are two associations serving the Palomino, and each has different registration requirements.

For more information: Palomino Horse Breeders of America, 15253 E. Skelly Drive, Tulsa, OK 74116-2637. Phone: 918-438-1234. Fax: 918-438-1232. E-mail: yellahorses@palominohba.com. Web: www.palominohba.com. Or Palomino Horse Association, HC 63, Box 24, Dornsife, PA 17823. Phone: 570-758-3067. Fax: 570-758-5336. E-mail: srebuck@mail.tds.net. Web: www.palominohorseassoc.com.

Pinto

The Pinto is also strictly a color breed with tobiano and overo (see Paint) spotting patterns.

The Pinto Horse Association of America was founded in 1947. Unlike the American Paint Horse Association, which registers horses based only on bloodlines of Paint, Quarter Horse, and Thoroughbred breeding, the PtHA welcomes spotted horses of all breeds, including ponies and Miniatures.

The PtHA categorizes horses and ponies according to conformation type and background: stock, hunter, pleasure, and saddle. Stock horse types are usually of Quarter Horse conformation and breeding. APHA horses are often eligible for this division. Hunter Pintos are generally of Thoroughbred, warmblood, or running Quarter Horse background. Pleasure Pintos are predominantly of Arabian or Morgan descent, and Saddle Pintos reflect American Saddlebred, Tennessee Walking Horse, or Missouri Fox Trotter breeding.

For more information: Pinto Horse Association of America, 1900 Samuels Avenue, Fort Worth, TX 76102-1141. Phone: 817-336-7842. Fax: 817-336-7416. E-mail: membership@pinto.org. Web: www.pinto.org.

Mules

One can't discuss trail-riding mounts and not mention mules. The mule is one of nature's oddities, a true hybrid. It's a cross between a horse and donkey. Because the mule inherits two numerically unmatched sets of chromosomes from its parents, it is sterile.

Thus, the only way you can get a mule is to breed a donkey jack to a mare or a stallion to a female donkey (jennet). The mule, generally speaking, picks up characteristics from both parents. It has the donkey's long ears, Roman nose, finer legs, and relatively small hooves and often the horse's larger body size, depending on the type of stallion or mare involved in the mating.

The resultant offspring from breeding a stallion to a jennet is called a hinny. Crossing a donkey jack on a mare produces the mule. The hinny is often finer boned and more horse-like than the mule.

The most popular jack stock used for breeding mules in this country is the mammoth American Standard Jack. Mammoth jacks are descended from Catalonian asses imported into the United States early in the nineteenth century.

I love using mules on the trail. They make excellent pack animals and are sure-footed mounts. Dealing with mules is different than dealing with horses. You rarely get anywhere with force. People who've tried to use force on mules probably coined the phrase: "Stubborn as a mule."

However, if you take the time to learn their personality traits, mules will provide many hours of trail-riding and packing pleasure.

What this really means is that mules are wonderful animals, but they aren't for everyone. One can't simply apply what one knows about horses to mules.

Some years ago I took two mares to a jack owner to be bred. The offspring would be the first mules I had ever owned.

The jack owner said to me: "I understand you train horses."

"Yes," I replied.

"You planning to train these mule colts after they're born?" he asked.

"I don't know why not," I replied. "Is there any reason I shouldn't consider doing that?"

"Oh," he said, "mules are different."

How right he was. I tried training the young mules as I routinely did young horses. It didn't work. I had to learn about mule psychology before I could achieve any success in the training program. This meant I had to talk to people who trained mules, and I read everything I could get my hands on. Only when I began to understand mule psychology could I effectively train the two youngsters.

If you want a mule, my advice would be buy one that has been trained to ride and pack. Then, you should talk with people who own, ride, and pack mules as part of the learning process in knowing and understanding these sometimes-complicated animals. If you make this effort and apply what you learn, the mule can be as good a trail companion as you'll ever own.

For more information: American Donkey and Mule Society, P.O. Box 1210, Lewisville, TX 75067. Phone: 972-219-0781. Fax: 972-420-9980. E-mail: adms@juno.com. Web: www.lovelongears.com.

2

HORSE PSYCHOLOGY
Why Horses Do What They Do

Understanding horse psychology is essential to understanding your trail horse's reactions to certain situations. What makes no sense to you may make perfect sense to your horse. For example, most horses don't like to enter small, dark spaces; walk through bogs; or cross streams. They've been programmed for millions of years to know that putting themselves in certain situations could mean danger and even death.

Perhaps the best way to learn about equine behavior and psychology is to observe horses in the wild. Obviously, that's not easy to do, but my wife, Linda, and I can give you the benefit of our experience. We had this opportunity — perhaps privilege is a better word — when we donated a young Arabian stallion to Theodore Roosevelt National Park in the North Dakota Badlands, near Medora. We made the donation at a time when park officials were worried about continued inbreeding in the wild bands that roamed the park. For the next ten years we traveled frequently to the Badlands to check on the maturing stallion and also to study wild horses in general.

What we learned about equine psychology from observing horses in the wild helped us understand our domestic horses better, especially our trail mounts.

Social Hierarchy

The first thing that's apparent in wild horses, and in domestic hors-

es, is a definitive pecking order. In every group one animal dominates. It goes on down the line from there. The number two horse
dominates number three and so on. Each horse knows and is comfortable with its position in the social hierarchy.

Interestingly, establishing the various positions in the pecking
order seldom involves major battles. Often it's done with a look or,
perhaps, a threatening gesture, such as laid-back ears or an aggressive approach. Once established, the pecking order remains until a
new horse is introduced into the group. If the new horse has domi-
neering tendencies, he might briefly battle the dominant horse.
Normally, it'll end quickly, and the loser will move into the number
two position and remain there. Rarely will the supplanted horse
challenge the dominant horse again.

This bit of equine psychology can help you with training. As a successful trainer or rider, you should establish, without abuse, your
dominance in the pecking order and take advantage of your horse's
willingness to submit. With trail riding, it is important that the horse
looks to you for security and leadership, especially when you come to
a spot that frightens the horse. By demonstrating gentle firmness, you

A social hierarchy exists among horses.

can convince the horse you know best and it is okay to go forward. If the horse feels he is in charge, he may balk and refuse to go on.

Lead Mare

In our youth most of us horse lovers read books and stories about wild stallions that could race like the wind, fight with fury, and lead their bands to safety when danger threatened.

While it's true that stallions control their bands, the lead mare actually handles most of the decision-making. The mare that establishes herself at the top of the pecking order, subservient only to the stallion, decides where the band grazes, when it goes to water, and at which water hole it drinks.

The lead mare becomes the dominant horse by convincing the other mares that she's tougher and stronger. She does this with posturing — pinning her ears and baring her teeth. If that doesn't work, she resorts to viciously snapping with her teeth and kicking with her rear feet. In every band there's always one female that ascends to lead mare and remains there.

The lead mare makes most of the decisions.

When it's time to go to the water hole, the lead mare sets off toward it, and the rest of the band strings out behind her, usually in pecking order.

The stallion usually brings up the rear, though the reason is unclear. Is it to urge stragglers to maintain the pace? Is it to guard against attacks from the rear? Or is he merely placing himself in the least vulnerable position, letting the mares and foals go first in case a predator waits along the pathway?

When the lead mare reaches the water, she's the first to drink. The others in the band take their turns, determined by pecking order. Sometimes the stallion will drink last, and sometimes he will shoulder his way through the group and be among the first to drink. When the herd has finished drinking, the lead mare finds a grazing spot or if it's late in the day, a sheltered spot where the band will spend the night.

Though the stallion is the dominant force in the band, he rarely questions the lead mare's decision.

You should seek leadership tendencies in your trail horse, be it mare, gelding, or stallion. Horses that are leaders are unafraid to be up front on a trail ride. They negotiate most obstacles without delay. This is important because if the lead horse stops, everyone down the line jams up. Generally speaking, the horse that is at the top, or near the top, of a group's pecking order will be the best trail mount.

Stallion As Protector

Occasionally a stallion abandons his customary position at the rear of the band and races to the front. Usually this occurs when the band encounters another stallion along the trail, particularly if it's during the spring breeding season.

The stallion may also move to the front if he perceives danger. One time when Linda and I were riding in the Badlands in search of our stallion, we encountered a band on its way to water. The lead mare spotted us instantly as the band rounded an outcropping. She stopped in her tracks, with the entire band halting behind her. She stared at us, her ears pricked forward and body poised for instant flight. The band's stallion — a big, rugged gray — raced to the front of the group and advanced toward us, blasting air through his nostrils in a challenging way. He was an imposing sight, but we sat quietly and held our ground. He approached to within seventy-five yards, giving himself a safety zone, then stopped and snorted again. Suddenly, he wheeled about and raced back toward his band. The moment the stallion turned away from us, the lead mare spun about and raced in the direction from which they had come, the entire band speeding after her. The stallion's action signaled that we represented a danger from which they should flee.

While wild stallions occasionally engage in vicious fights for herd supremacy, dominance is usually established with simple posturing.

We witnessed this during an interesting confrontation between the stallion we had donated and another wild stallion. Our stallion had quickly adopted the behaviors of a wild stallion, accumulating a small band of mares. As we watched from a hiding place, we saw a large roan stallion approach the band. Our stallion, much smaller in stature, went forward to meet him. The two horses came nose to nose, sniffing each other. Without warning, our stallion squealed, spun in his tracks, and kicked the larger horse in the chest with his rear hooves.

The challenging stallion, though much larger and more powerful, merely turned and walked away. The fight ended before it began, and the larger horse was uninjured. It appeared he could have

Stallions often battle for herd supremacy.

whipped his smaller and younger counterpart but, instead, had decided our stallion was the dominant one and left.

What all of this tells us as trail riders is that a stallion's role in the wild is to protect his band from intruders and breed mares. He is responsible in large part for propagation of the species. Even when domesticated, the stallion's focus in life is on reproduction. As a result, many stallions are not suitable trail mounts. A mare in the trail-riding group that happens to be in heat could become the stallion's focus, rather than walking or trotting along in a calm manner.

To be sure, there are excellent trail-riding stallions that seem to shut down their hormones while under saddle, but they are the exceptions. Normally, one is better served with a mare or gelding as a trail horse.

Accepting Change

As already mentioned, most horses accept change in the pecking order quite readily when a new horse is introduced into the group. Again, we saw this demonstrated in the wild with our donated stallion. During his maturing years our stallion successfully formed and maintained a small band of mares. Then disaster struck. He became tangled in a string of barbed wire that lay hidden in grass, probably a carryover from earlier days when parts of the Badlands had been homesteaded.

The stallion seriously injured his left rear leg, with the wire cutting into the tendon, but not severing it. Park personnel captured him and took him to a ranch to heal. Another stallion quickly gathered up his mares. After our horse recovered, park rangers returned him to the wild. We didn't see what happened, but the wounds on his neck and back let us know that he had challenged the other stallion in an effort to reacquire his mares.

He lost the battle, perhaps in part because he didn't have full use of one rear leg. The interesting part to us was that he stayed with the band, becoming the number two stallion. He remained in that position until a change in park policy resulted in his being removed. Ten years after we donated the stallion, the park service decided that inbreeding wasn't a problem. They gathered up the introduced horses and many of their offspring and sold them at auction. We bought "our" horse at that auction, and he remained with us until he died of natural causes.

The message here is that horses adapt to change. The trail horse that attempts to dominate you will submit quickly once it learns that you are number one in its pecking order.

Fierce When Threatened

As with nearly all wild creatures, mares fiercely protect their young. Their first instinct to avoid perceived danger is flight, but if that doesn't work, they're often prepared to fight. This instinct remains in domestic mares. If you decide to breed your good female trail horse and raise a foal, you need to keep this instinct in mind. It could mean that she will not be a steady mount until the foal has been weaned.

I can attest that a threatened mare with a foal is not to be taken lightly. I bred my Quarter Horse cutting mare and eagerly awaited the foal's arrival. I checked her early one morning and sure enough, there was the little colt I knew was going to set the cutting world on fire. In my

A mare instinctively protects her foal.

excitement I rushed right into the stall. After all, this mare was always very calm and docile. Not this morning! She flattened her ears, bared her teeth, and lunged at me. I beat a hasty retreat. She couldn't flee from the stall, but her basic instincts told her she could fight off a perceived attacker. In a couple of days when the colt was bopping around the stall and corral, she relaxed and became her old easygoing self again.

While on the trail, some riders allow the foal to trot along. This can be a problem, especially if the mare is overly protective. She will become agitated if the foal is out of sight and may turn teeth and heels on another horse she feels is getting too close to her foal.

The Role of Genetics

Genetics play a prominent role in temperament and the presence of neuroses. This doesn't mean that because a horse's dam was a cribber (wind sucker) — an animal that grips a solid object with its teeth and sucks air into its stomach — the offspring will do the same. However, it does mean the offspring may very well inherit a nervous disposition that finds its outlet in some sort of neuroses, perhaps wind sucking.

It's important that we pay as much attention to a horse's emotional makeup as we do to its physical structure. As mentioned, some horses have trouble with confinement. If you keep such a horse locked in a box stall for long hours, it will likely develop one vice or another. Some will paw. Others will weave from side to side. Others will kick the sides of the stall or gnaw on wood and/or become cribbers.

Unfortunately, vices that stem from such neuroses very often remain with the horse for life. Your goal must be to understand your horse's emotional needs and take steps to prevent it from developing neurotic behavior.

Primal Fears

Horses are blessed (or cursed, depending on your point of view) with instincts that have allowed the species to survive thousands of years. The ability to perceive danger is one of them. For example, when wild horses travel across their chosen terrain, they'll almost always go around obstacles rather than through them. They'll go to a water hole to drink, for example, but rarely will they walk through a water-filled or marshy area unless forced by fear or human pressure.

Trail riders should be aware of the reason. Through the years horses have developed fears that will likely stay with them for all time. In the earlier days a number of large predators ate horses. In their ongoing struggle to prevent becoming a large cat's evening meal, horses took off. Their instincts told them if they became bogged down in a marshy area, they would be unable to flee, so they avoided such areas at all costs.

The innate fear of being trapped in mud remains with the domesticated horse. Knowing this primal instinct should help you understand why many horses hate to cross water, particularly if the bank of the stream or pond is muddy or marshy.

The same is true of a horse having weight and strange objects, such as a rider, placed on its back. Some predators, such as big cats, attacked from overhanging branches, dropping onto the victim's back, digging in with claws, and then breaking the horse's neck with its powerful jaws. With that in mind, it's no mystery why many young horses become agitated when a rider steps aboard for the first time.

Many horses have an instinctive fear of water.

Horses in the wild almost never jump over an object if there's any way to get around it. Jumping can cause injury, and injury in the wild often is synonymous with death. Horses also have a blind spot and lose sight of the object they're about to jump just before they become airborne.

Closed-in places can be traps, preventing a horse from fleeing, thus spelling disaster in the wild. This knowledge helps you understand why your horses are reluctant to get into a trailer until you convince them that no harm will result from the confinement.

You can't prevent your horse from having these fears. However, if you use appropriate training methods, you can condition your horse to obey and trust you, even though its instincts tell it to do otherwise.

Adapt or Die

Going from wild to domestic has been a huge adaptation for horses. Just being able to get over the innate fears mentioned above is a major step in the development of any horse. How easily those fears are conquered depends on the horse's emotional tendencies and stability.

Some can't handle confinement. Others can't stand pressure during training or are nervous and flighty, spooking at even a minor disturbance in their environment.

Your goal, of course, is to own and ride a trail horse that can adapt to a changing environment and accept you as the dominant figure in its life without being afflicted with neurotic tendencies.

The Equine Intellect

While it's difficult to measure equine intelligence, there's little doubt that some horses are smarter than others. Some horses learn and respond quickly, making them a pleasure to train, while others seem incapable of learning and responding to basic stimuli.

Horses, by the way, are capable of latent learning. I have seen this over and over with young horses. I've had occasions where I seemed to hit a wall in a youngster's training and have simply turned it out for several weeks. When I brought the horse back in and resumed training, not only had it remembered everything it'd been taught, but had also mastered and moved past whatever it was that had stopped previous progress.

The fact that horses have good memories can be both a blessing and a curse. The curse surfaces when the horse has had a traumatic experience. In some cases that experience remains embedded in its psyche for life, and whenever similar circumstances arise, the horse becomes frightened and traumatized all over again. This memory capability can also result in the development of bad habits. If, for example, a horse becomes agitated and pulls back while tied, it may be the precursor for serious problems, more so if the lead line or halter should break. That horse may well remember forever that it got free by pulling back and will continue to do so.

Because the horse has an excellent memory, especially when trauma is involved, it's imperative that the training program for your trail horse be slow and steady, with one positive experience serving as a steppingstone for another.

There are, however, horses that simply don't want to submit to a training regimen. They have adapted to living in a world inhabited by humans but do not want to yield to any of their demands. Avoid a horse with this psychological makeup because it'll resist anything new.

Horses Understand Respect

Many horse owners want to believe that their horses respond to love and affection the way a dog does. The equine world doesn't work that way. Horses respect, and trust, what they consider a dominant figure, but rarely do they display canine-type affection. If you have been gone for a day or two, your favorite dog will likely be overjoyed at your return, barking and leaping in its ecstasy. If you are gone for a few days and go out into the pasture to check on your horse, it might stroll up to you, but its motive, for the most part, will be to see if you're bringing it a treat.

This does not mean that horses are blank, unfeeling creatures that can't differentiate between good treatment and bad. It merely means that horses rarely have a "love" relationship with humans.

That being said, horses, when being trained or ridden, often respond better to one person than to another. I've seen horses difficult for men to train and handle become putty in a woman's hands. Perhaps the horse was timid by nature and the woman was less aggressive or had softer hands.

It can also go the other way. A horse with a dominant, type-A personality can take advantage of every weakness shown by its human handler. Soon the horse is the dominant figure, and the human, male or female, is in the number two spot. This is dangerous for the human, because if a thousand-pound horse no longer respects its handler, injury waits in the wings.

This horse needs a more aggressive, strong-willed person to be in charge. Back when I was training horses for other people, I hated to see this type of horse come into the stable. It wasn't so much that I couldn't get the horse to respond to me and do all the things its owner desired. Not at all. The problem was that the "cure" was usually short-lived. When the horse returned home, it would be only a matter of time before it once again exerted its will over a timid rider, only this time with perhaps a new wrinkle added.

MAKING SENSE OF THE SENSES
How a Horse's Eyes and Ears Affect Its Behavior on the Trail

It's all in the eye of the beholder. That cliché has been around for years, but when we consider it in light of the human eye compared to the equine eye, the saying takes on a whole different meaning.

Humans and horses literally see things differently, and this difference can sometimes lead to problems on the trail. No doubt you've ridden on windy days when suddenly your horse became agitated and excited. A piece of paper flew across the road or trail and your horse jumped or stopped dead in its tracks. This might well be the same horse you rode on this trail yesterday without a hint of skittishness.

Why the sudden change in behavior? Because of the way your horse sees. Once you learn how the equine eye functions, you'll better understand your horse's actions. And you'll have insight managing your trail horse when it becomes skittish for no apparent reason.

Let's consider the windy day–flying paper scenario. You didn't give a second thought to that piece of paper skittering across the trail. Your horse, though, saw a strange, out-of-focus object moving across its path. The inability of your horse's eye to send a clear message to the brain brought on apprehension and fear.

The fear of unidentified moving objects comes from being a prey animal. For centuries equines served as tasty meals for big cats and other predators. Some would lie in wait or up in a tree for a horse to pass by and then spring to the attack. In other, rarer cases, the pred-

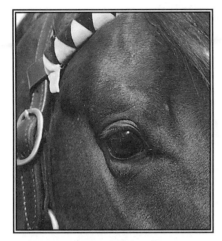
Horses see things differently.

ator simply outran the horse and dragged it down for the kill.

Whatever the case, the horse knew sudden movement meant danger.

However, Mother Nature did not leave the horse defenseless against predators. She blessed the horse with an unusually broad field of vision, keen hearing, the ability to lash out with front and back hooves and, most importantly, the ability to outdistance all but the fastest of pursuers.

Unique Eye

The equine eye is unique in that it has both monocular and binocular vision. With monocular vision, the horse can see objects with one eye. As a result the brain often is receiving two images at the same time, sort of like a human attempting to watch side-by-side television sets simultaneously and absorb the action on both. With binocular vision, however, the horse can see the same object with both eyes at the same time and only one message is conveyed to the brain. A horse's eyes are wide apart and on each side of its head to accommodate monocular vision better — very important to a prey animal, as we'll see.

Humans have only binocular vision. We fall into the predator rather than the prey category. As such, our eyes are in the front of the head, and only a short distance apart, just like other predators — lions, tigers, dogs, and cats. A predator's eyes are designed to focus on the prey it's attempting to chase down.

Therefore, we can quickly focus on objects while the horse, with its broader range of vision, has trouble bringing things into focus.

Auto-Focusing

The human eye is a lot like an auto-focus camera, making use of disc-like lenses that are attached to powerful ciliary muscles. These muscles quickly flex or relax to adjust the lens shape as needed. If you want to look at something far away, you simply stare at the object and, in a flash, the lens focuses on it and you see it with clarity. If the object is close, the same thing happens, only the focal point is much nearer.

If you want to look at something to either the right or left, you simply turn your head and the ciliary muscles do the rest, sending a sharp image to the retina, a mass of nerve receptors on your eyeball's back wall. The retina then transmits the image to the brain — all in the proverbial blink of an eye.

Compared with a human's ciliary muscles, the horse's are underdeveloped and do a poor job of bringing objects into focus. There's also a big difference in the retina. In humans the retina is a smooth, concave surface. The equine retina is more concave in some places than in others, and some sections are nearer the cornea than others. (The cornea is that transparent structure at the front of the eye that covers the iris and pupil and admits light to the interior.)

Difficulty Focusing

Because the horse can't focus on objects as we do, it compensates by lifting and lowering or weaving its head from side to side. It may also try to get either farther away from or closer to an object to bring it into focus.

Even when the horse has focused as best it can, its sight

Focusing is difficult for horses.

is only three-fifths that of a human. In other words, when looking at an object twenty feet away, the horse sees only as much detail as a person with twenty-twenty vision would if the object were thirty-five feet away.

This means, of course, that when you're riding down the trail and see a strange object ahead, you'll recognize what you're seeing long before your horse does.

Monocular Vision

Because its eyes are large — the largest of any land mammal — and on each side of its skull, the horse has a very broad field of vision. A horse actually has a vision field of more than 350 degrees, compared to the less than 180 degrees in the human.

Only about 65 degrees of the horse's field of vision are binocular — seen with both eyes — while the remaining 285 degrees are monocular — seen with one eye.

Flight Instinct

Poor focusing ability is the reason fleeing is one of the horse's strongest instincts. When the horse's brain receives confusing

Flight is the horse's primary instinct.

images because the eyes are unable to focus clearly on an object, the horse calls on its primary instinct, evading that object until it can be better identified.

The horse's composite field of vision of more than 350 degrees results in two cone-shaped blind spots — one directly in front when the horse is within about four feet of an object and the other directly behind. The rear blind spot is eight to ten feet in length.

Keeping the horse's front blind spots in mind, you can easily understand why your horse may run into a log or other object that you ask it to step over immediately after rounding a corner. The horse must first see the object before it's lost in the blind spot, know where the object is even though it can't be seen, and then decide that it poses no danger.

I constantly marvel at Grand Prix jumpers that sail over six-foot fences because the fences are lost in the blind spot before the horse ever launches itself into the air.

While you can focus on objects more clearly than your horse, it can pick up motion more quickly. My wife and I learned a lot about equine vision during the years we studied the wild horses of Theodore Roosevelt National Park. (See Chapter 2, "Horse Psychology.") If we could clearly view them without being seen and remain still, the horses never noticed us though they might be grazing nearby. If we made the slightest movement, however, their heads shot up, their ears pricked forward, and their eyes were on us.

Whether in the wild or on the trail, it's rare for a horse to focus on a still object, particularly in the distance.

Moving Objects

Sometimes when Linda and I would move, the wild horses would take off at a run. At other times they would actually trot toward us, trying all the while to get us into sharper focus. The horses, after moving toward or away from us, would stop and hold their heads in a more perpendicular fashion as part of their effort to get the retina adjusted for better focus.

We are all familiar with the far-sighted person who uses the magnifying portion of bifocal eyeglasses to read but looks over the top of the magnifiers to identify who just drove up. A horse's eyeballs operate similarly to bifocal glasses. This makes sense because the horse is a grazing creature. When its head is lowered and it's looking through the upper portion of its eyes, it can continually survey the horizon for predators. If there's something up close that demands its attention, the horse will examine the object through the lower portion of its eyes.

Here's another example of how the equine eye works: You're riding along a trail that crosses an open meadow with your steady mount picking its way in ground-covering but unhurried fashion. A deer flashes from cover on a hillside several hundred yards in front of you. Your eyes immediately focus on the moving object as your lenses adjust in a flash, and you know instantly that it's a deer.

Your horse will likely have picked up the flash of movement before you did, but that's about all it would have been able to discern at that distance. It would not be unusual for the horse to come to a stop and tip its head perpendicular so that it could use its binocular vision via the upper half of the eyeball to get the moving deer into focus.

A veteran trail horse will either get the running deer into focus or

Horses' eyes work like bifocal glasses.

trust you, providing you remain calm and relaxed in the saddle. If your horse is a green trail mount, unused to varying sights and motions on the trail, the horse might remain tense and edgy until well past the spot where you first saw the deer. How you react at a time like this will have a bearing on a young or novice trail horse's attitude. If you become tense, your horse will know it and remain convinced there is something to fear. If, however, you sit calmly and urge your horse forward at a quiet walk, it will draw on your confidence and relax.

Here's something else to ponder when you wonder why your horse acts as it does on a trail ride. Remember that the horse has the largest eye of any land mammal. This means it also has an oversized retina. What all this boils down to is that the horse's eyes magnify objects.

If a dog bolts out of a driveway and begins snapping or yapping at your horse, the equine eye might magnify the animal to appear far more formidable and fearsome than it is. To your eyes, it will just be a dog; to your horse's, it might appear as large as a small pony.

In addition, if the dog is running from one side of the horse to the other, first one eye sees the animal and reports to the brain and then the other eye does likewise. Now, the horse is receiving two messages about the troublesome dog, and the result may well be a somewhat confused and fractious mount prancing from side to side to keep the creature in focus.

Being Two-Sided

Because your horse has monocular vision, it's important that you train it to be "two-sided." Here's what I mean. If you're working a horse in a corral or arena and are going to the left, the horse is seeing any activity in the center of the ring or arena with its left eye. The horse will be curious, maybe even tense, in the beginning, but then will relax. When you turn to the right and begin circling, you may wonder why the horse has become curious and tense again. Seeing the activity in the center ring through its right eye has sent a whole new set of signals to its brain.

The same problem arises with mounting, dismounting, and leading the horse. You want your trail horse to accept being mounted and dismounted from either side and to be led from either side. The day might come when you're in the mountains and need to dismount in a spot where there's either no room on the left or perhaps a steep drop-off. Having the horse panic when you dismount from the right side for the first time could be disastrous in such a situation.

Seeing in the Dark

Though it may have trouble getting objects into focus, the equine eye, because of its size, is vastly superior to the human eye in one important respect — a horse can see far better in the dark. Generally speaking, a horse's night vision is about 50 percent better than ours.

I remember a trek into the mountains of Bridger-Teton National Forest in Wyoming that proved the point. I was riding a solid-going Thoroughbred gelding. We had run into some problems on the return trip after several days of camping, and darkness overtook our group before we could reach our base camp. I was in front on the gelding, leading part of the pack string, with the rest of the group following.

Clouds covered the sky, so neither stars nor moon shed light. It was so dark I couldn't see the trail. I had to trust the horse. I dropped the reins and let my horse pick his own way. That big gelding led us down the twisting, sometimes difficult trail without missing a step.

How could he do that when I couldn't see where we were going?

Basically, because the horse has much more light to work with than we do. A structure at the back of the eye, the tapetum lucidum, reflects light through the eye, making the horse's eyes appear to shine in the dark; thus, in effect, the light is used twice.

Second, a horse's pupils are horizontal, allowing them to dilate much more than our circular pupils. This means more light can enter the horse's eye in the dark.

A third reason for the horse's superior night vision is its much larger cornea.

The horse simply has more light to work with at night than we do.

Objects may appear even more out of focus to the horse than in daylight, but at least it can see far better than we can where it's setting its feet.

Understanding how the equine eye functions is essential if you're to understand why your trail horse does what it does in varying circumstances. It also should be clear that good vision is essential in your trail horses and that you, as the owner, should be conscious of potential injury or disease that can compromise their eyesight.

The Window to the Horse's Soul

A horse's eyes give us insight into its personality and way of thinking. If you study equine behavior, you'll soon learn to discern the difference between a calm eye, which denotes an even disposition, and an angry eye or one filled with worry and concern.

An old myth says that if you can see the white of a horse's eye, you should beware because it indicates a mean temperament. That's not true. Often, the white that shows is merely the way the eyeball is constructed and fits into the socket. Some horses simply lack pigment in that area. Sclera, or white around the cornea, is common in the Appaloosa and doesn't mean the horses are ill-tempered.

On the other hand, if a horse's eye normally shows no white, it is usually a sign of agitation when it does.

The calm eye is just that. It has an almost sleepy quality with little movement. An apprehensive eye has much more movement and will have a startled look. The angry eye will narrow and focus on the object of its displeasure — often you, the rider.

All Ears

Equines hear much better than humans. Their ears, with their length and concave structure, are perfectly shaped to gather sound. While this auditory capability serves survival purposes in the wild, it can be a detriment when you are trail riding on a windy day or when a particularly noisy car, truck, or motorcycle thunders past on a country road. What sounds normal to you might be a mind-numbing roar to your horse.

If you're riding down a tree- or brush-lined trail when the wind is blowing, your ears record what, by comparison, is a muted sound and your eyes send distinct images to the brain of waving branches and brush. Your horse's ears pick up a confusing cacophony of sound, and its eyes send the brain indistinct images of a mass of moving objects.

A horse that may have been a quiet ride on a Saturday afternoon with no wind becomes jumpy and agitated over the same trail on Sunday when the wind is blowing.

In addition to gathering sound, your horse's ears let you know what's going on in its mind. When alert and curious, your horse will walk with its ears forward. When angry or sullen, it might point them to the rear. If you mount your trail horse and it pins its ears and begins swishing its tail in an aggravated manner, be careful. It's telling you that it's unhappy and just might be preparing to remove you from its back.

4

TEMPERAMENT
Buying the Right Horse for the Trail

If you're going to enjoy trail riding, you need a horse with a good temperament. You may have the best-conformed horse in the world, with sound limbs and body, but that will matter little if the horse is mentally and emotionally unsuited for the trail.

The right match is important.

In a discussion of proper temperament in a trail horse, words like "solid" and "steady" come to mind. You want a horse that will carry you over a trail with little to no fuss or fidgeting — a horse that is solid and steady in the bridle, even when distracted.

The following are some common traits to look for in a good trail horse, and some traits to avoid. This chapter also includes how you can test a prospective mount to determine its suitability for the trail.

A note to the beginning rider: if you want to get a horse so you can learn to ride, it's a good idea to take some riding lessons first. Go to a reputable stable and ask to ride a variety of horses so you can learn to tell the difference in both riding comfort and temperament.

Once you're comfortable riding and have decided what kind of trail-riding horse you want, you're ready to shop.

Being Alert

We've all heard trail riders say with pride: "My horse will go over or through anything."

On the surface that sounds like the temperament you want. However, good temperament is a little more complicated and subtle. Yes, it just may be fine if a horse steps right over a log and pays no attention to the large brown object beside the trail. But what if that log partially covered a crumbling hole or what if that brown object turned out to be a snoozing bear? Then you'd want the horse to give pause and take a second look at where it's going. Look for a horse that's alert to its surroundings and pays special attention to unusual objects. This is where the subtlety comes in. You want the horse to be observant, but you don't want it to become agitated and frightened when it sees something unusual.

If the horse encounters something that it fears and wishes to avoid, its reaction is either to go around it or leave the scene. In such situations you want a horse with a quiet, trusting temperament — one that will let you overrule its instincts and will go forward instead of fleeing.

That being said, for every rule there's an exception. There are times when the horse's instincts are right. One of my best trail mounts was an Arabian gelding. Together we covered miles up and down mountains, along country roads, and across flat land. He was always alert, with ears pricked forward; and he walked on with a nice, long stride.

When I purchased him, he was well broke but hadn't been ridden on trails much. The first water puddle we encountered caused him to panic. All he needed, however, was a steady hand and reassurance, and within a short time he lost his fear of water.

I was riding him on one of our mountain excursions when we came to a stream. The bridge had broken down and couldn't be used.

While the rest of the group waited, I looked for another crossing. I found one just downstream. The ground looked solid, and the water was not more than belly deep. To make sure, I decided to cross the stream alone before leading the rest of the group.

My gelding got to within a yard or so of the water and wouldn't take another step. I was both surprised and upset. After that initial episode at a water puddle some years earlier, he had never refused me. I urged him more firmly, but he would not budge.

I decided at this point that maybe he knew something I didn't. I dismounted, walked to the edge of the stream, and found myself floundering in soft, squishy mud completely camouflaged with green grass and leaves. It had looked like solid ground to me. My horse had known better. I never doubted him after that.

If he'd been a horse that would blindly go wherever I pointed him, we would have been in deep trouble. We did find a safe crossing farther downstream.

Good in a Group

When you are riding with others, your position in the group should not be a problem for your horse. A good trail horse should be a solid leader, walk along quietly in the middle of the pack, or bring up the rear without getting out of sorts. You definitely don't want a horse that must always be in front. It's no fun to hold back a jigging, almost uncontrollable horse that wants to be first in line. Neither do you want a horse that lags behind so much you have to trot constantly to keep up.

A good, well-mannered trail horse gets along with other horses. Stay away from the

A good trail horse maintains his place.

surly horse that flattens its ears and swishes its tail whenever another horse approaches. When a horse shows this type of temper, it's only a matter of time before it kicks or bites another horse that happens to be coming up behind or passing by.

Nothing will make you more unpopular on a group trail ride than to be mounted on a horse that bites and kicks. Some organized trail rides require such horses to wear a red ribbon in their tails to warn approaching riders. Unfortunately, that doesn't solve anything. The horse that kicks must be taught that this is inappropriate behavior. If that doesn't work, it's time to look for another trail mount unless you always ride alone.

Buddying Up

Avoid a horse that constantly buddies up to other horses. Such a horse will practically run over others to get next to a pal that has gone ahead.

I once had a mare we used both for the trail and the show ring. All it would take for her to buddy up with another horse was to travel somewhere in the same trailer. We discovered this penchant for instant fellowship when my daughter competed in a 4-H show. We hauled the mare and a horse belonging to my daughter's friend in the same trailer.

Some horses form strong attachments.

Our mare was instantly in love.

The two girls were in the same class, and when they were traveling along the rail across the ring from each other, my daughter's mare looked longingly at her newfound friend and began to whinny. The mare's whinnying was an expression of her desire to be in close proximity to her companion.

The only solution was to separate her and her traveling companion immediately upon arriving at the show ground. If they were tethered apart, there was less of a problem.

A good friend of mine had a mare and gelding pastured together and, in the gelding's mind, the two were inseparable. When the two horses were ridden in a group on a trail ride, the gelding had to be directly behind that mare or he was impossible to ride. There was one advantage to this distracting problem. My friend could ride the mare and mount an inexperienced rider on the gelding. He never had to worry whether the horse was giving the rider a problem because the gelding was always right behind and would follow the mare anywhere without question.

Nervous horses usually stay that way.

The Nervous Horse

The poorest candidate for a trail horse is one that's flighty and nervous — the horse that's afraid of everything. You can make some progress with horses of this type, but, generally speaking, they're going to stay that way.

You can get them used to passing a fallen tree or large boulder along the trail without shying if you expose them to the same object over and over, but when you ride a new trail with different scary objects, the problem resurfaces and you have to go through the same procedure.

Nervous, flighty horses can be dangerous. It might not seem like a big deal when your horse jumps sideways from what it perceives to be a scary object, but when the same thing happens on a mountain trail with a steep drop-off, the outcome could be disastrous.

Another recipe for disaster is a nervous, high-strung horse ridden by a nervous, high-strung rider. The mental match-up between horse and rider is as important as the physical one.

It's far better to buy a horse with a solid, steady temperament than to try to train the animal to overcome its nervousness. You'll fail at that endeavor far more often than you'll ever succeed.

The terms "solid and steady," however, do not mean lazy. You don't want a horse that's so laid back it hates to move out of its tracks. While trying to control a flighty horse can be wearing, the same is true of attempting to maintain a steady pace with a dull horse that only wants to stop and stand.

Look for a horse with a solid, steady temperament.

Finding the Right Horse

If you're shopping for a good trail mount and you're not an experienced horse person, ask for help, even if you have to pay for it. Having a professional help you evaluate a horse will likely turn out to be a bargain in the long run. A person who works with horses for a living can usually read a horse's temperament very quickly.

The first step is to find a horse. You can peruse the classifieds in the daily newspaper or your region's local horse publication, search the Web, check the local feed and tack store bulletin boards, or ask around. But perhaps a better way is to work with a professional who is familiar with horses and owners in the area.

Checking Out the Horse

Once you have located a potential purchase, make an appointment to evaluate the horse. Make certain the owner or someone who has worked with the horse is present when you arrive. Discussing the horse with someone who knows little or nothing about it will not be helpful. Let the owner or trainer know you're interested in a solid trail horse and want to see it ridden facing some conditions you'd find on a trail.

Ask to see the horse without its saddle first. That way you and your professional helper will have an opportunity to inspect the horse for any faults or blemishes. Once you've examined the horse and determined there are no serious faults, ask that it be saddled.

Watch carefully as the horse is saddled. Does it stand quietly? Does it roll its eyes nervously or pin its ears? How about when the

Watch how the horse accepts the bridle.

cinch is drawn tight? Does the horse expand its belly? These are sure signs that saddling and riding have been sour experiences. You're looking for a horse that stands still while being saddled and cinched, whose ears move forward and back to monitor what's going on.

Next, watch the horse being bridled. This is a simple but very important step. Does the horse shut its mouth and raise its head, like a giraffe, to avoid the bit? This is a serious fault that often worsens with time. What you want is a horse that keeps its head level or even lowers it and opens its mouth to accept the bit. Observe also when the horse is unbridled. It should open its mouth so the bit falls free.

When it comes time to ride, you want the owner or the person showing the horse to ride first so you can observe its behavior. Does the horse stand quietly while the rider mounts or does it fidget and turn in circles? A good trail horse stands quietly and remains standing until cued to move forward. Once the rider is aboard, does the horse walk off quietly with its ears forward or is it agitating the bit and tossing its head? The latter is definitely a sign that the horse is nervous about the whole procedure, and this anxiousness can make

The horse should stand quietly when being mounted.

the ride miserable. Also, the horse does not have respect for the rider's leadership and thinks it's in charge.

Next ask the rider to demonstrate the horse's gaits, moving from the walk to the trot and from the trot to the lope. Does the horse hold to a steady walk until asked to trot, or does it prance along with short, mincing steps? When the rider asks for the next gear, does the horse trot off straight and true or does it surge into the bit, attempting to break into a gallop? When the rider asks for a lope, does the horse effortlessly shift gears or does it leap into a run with the rider desperately attempting to rein it in?

While this activity is going on, watch the horse's eyes and ears. They're great attitude barometers. The happy horse will focus on the route ahead with its ears either forward or working back and forth. Rolling eyes and pinned ears mean an unhappy, unstable horse.

In summary, the horse you're looking for should stand quietly while being mounted, move off at a steady flat-footed walk, trot at a ground-covering but unhurried pace, move effortlessly into the lope while traveling along on a light rein, and look happy doing it.

Barn Sour

A barn-sour horse is one that refuses to leave the barn area, and/or when you turn it for home, heads back at speed, regardless of what you want.

A good test for this problem is to ask the owner or trainer to ride the horse away from the place, then to lope halfway back, rein in the horse, and walk the rest of the way. The barn-sour horse will not want to walk back and will fidget and lean into the bit.

This is a bad habit that

Consider the horse's attitude.

is both dangerous and difficult to break, especially if the rider is a novice. I know of cases where barn-sour horses have raced back to a stable and through an open doorway, almost decapitating their riders.

More Tests

Find out whether the horse will walk through water without coercion. If need be, a puddle can be created with a water hose. You want a horse that will look at the water and go through it without extraordinary urging.

The horse should also negotiate obstacles on the trail with ease. Ask the demonstrator to ride the horse over a log or something that will simulate a log, such as a small pile of boards. A good trail horse will drop its head to examine the obstacle and then step over it carefully.

Also ask the demonstrator to approach the obstacle at a trot or lope and see if the horse will jump it. Give the horse pluses for hopping over the obstacle without hesitation.

Find out if a horse will walk willingly through water.

To help determine the horse's reliability, check its reactions to windy conditions. Tell the demonstrator you want to find out if the horse shies from fluttering objects. A good way to do this is to tie a piece of plastic (like a garbage bag) to a tree or fence post and have the horse ridden by it.

There will also be times that a sudden storm arises, and you'll be scrambling for a raincoat. Sometimes it'll be inconvenient to dismount to don the rain gear. Ask the rider to put on and remove a raincoat while in the saddle. The good trail horse should stand quietly while this is going on.

When being ridden along a busy road or highway, the good trail horse should also pay little heed to motorized vehicles. The ultimate test is a noisy motorcycle, which because of its narrow shape and rapid movement is difficult for the horse to bring into proper focus. The same is true of a bicycle, minus the noise. If a motorcycle isn't available, at least ask that someone ride past the horse on a bicycle. Someone should also drive past the horse with a car or truck. A pickup pulling a rattling trailer is another good test.

Noise is disconcerting to horses because of their acute sense of hearing. However, the good trail horse should be immune to loud, harsh noises. Test the horse by banging a garbage can lid or some other noise-producing object with a stick as the horse is ridden past you.

After the demonstration ask the rider to stop but remain mounted for a time. You want to see if the horse will stand quietly and not dance around or fidget. There are many times you will want to stop to visit with another rider or simply enjoy the scenery. Those precious moments can be lost if your horse won't stand still.

Ask the rider to back the horse. It should continue to step backward as long as the rider applies give-and-release pressure to its mouth. The horse shouldn't lock up and refuse to move — not a good trait for trail riding.

Passing the above tests in a quiet, steady manner is a "must" for any trail horse candidate. The following are other tests that would fit into the "very good, but not absolutely necessary" category.

Other Tests

The ability of a horse to respond in a positive manner to leg and rein cues is a strong indication that an animal has been well trained and will be a responsive trail-riding companion.

For example, it's more convenient to have a horse you don't have to dismount to open the many gates you find on the trail. Ask the person who's demonstrating the horse to side-pass up to a gate, unlatch it, and push it open. Consider it a strong plus, though not necessarily a requirement, if the horse will do this and also side-pass back to the gate so that the rider can close it.

You also might want to know how well the horse reacts to other forms of leg pressure. Can the rider use his legs to cue the horse to

move its rear quarters in a circle while shifting the front feet just enough to enable the movement, but not going forward or rearward? This is called turning on the forehand. Conversely, will the horse anchor its rear feet, moving them just enough to allow it to complete a circle with the front end? This is called a turn on the backhand or hindquarters. While being able to do

Assess the horse's gaits.

this should not be considered essential, it is a definite sign that the horse has been well trained.

Checking the Gaits

Having a trail horse with a ground-covering, solid walk can't be over-emphasized. The most uncomfortable horse to ride is one that walks three steps and then trots two, walks five steps and then trots four — what I call "jiggle trotting." In some cases, conformation won't allow the horse to walk fast enough to keep up. But in many other cases, it's merely a matter of a horse being too fidgety to maintain a steady pace.

If possible, ask that the horse be demonstrated with another horse. There is also nothing wrong with hauling a second horse (hopefully one with a good, long stride) to where you're testing the candidate. Ask that the candidate be ridden beside this horse. Does the candidate stretch its stride to keep up while maintaining the walk, or does it consistently trot a few steps and walk a few steps? Your trail horse doesn't have to be the fastest walker in the world, but it should be able to lengthen its stride to cover ground rapidly and efficiently. If the candidate can't keep up, it should not break into a trot but continue at its maximum walking pace even though the other horse moves ahead.

It's also wise to make certain a potential purchase will allow its feet to be picked up and worked on. Ask the owner to demonstrate.

Your Turn

After the horse has been demonstrated to your satisfaction, it's your turn. Get on the horse and give it a try. Again, it's time to take inventory. Does the horse stand quietly for you, a stranger, to mount it? Does it respond quickly to your signals? Are the gaits comfortable? Is it relaxed and quiet, yet eager to go forward?

Most importantly, do you begin to feel a rapport with the horse after riding a short time?

The Final Test

Hopefully, you'll be able to give the prospective trail mount the final test before making up your mind — a real trail ride. In some cases you may be lucky enough to find a place on or near the seller's property where you can ride the horse under real trail conditions. Have the owner or his rider/trainer accompany you on this outing so he can explain how the horse has been trained to handle certain situations or obstacles.

If riding on the owner's property is not possible, perhaps you will be allowed to take the horse home for a short trial. I have a good friend who deals heavily in buying and selling trail horses. He always insists that the potential buyer take the horse home and use it for three or four days or even a week before making a decision. His instructions are, "Take him home and ride him. If he doesn't work out, bring him back, and we'll find you another one." That approach is ideal. You can put the horse to various tests and, most important- ly, find out whether your temperament matches the horse's.

Actually, that approach is good for both buyer and seller. The buyer has an opportunity to give the horse a serious tryout; and the seller knows he has a satisfied customer who will spread the good word. A host of satisfied customers is the key reason my trader friend does the volume of business he does.

Age and Temperament

A factor that can affect temperament is age. Many trail horses don't really mature mentally and physically until they are seven or older. If you're a beginning trail rider, it might be wise to start with a veteran trail horse that has earned a reputation as a dependable mount.

About the worst thing a beginner can do is purchase a young horse so the two of them can learn together. It is far better to find that dependable horse that will be your steady companion and teacher as you travel the trails together.

5

CONFORMATION
Being Built to Last

In discussing a horse's physical make up, or conformation, most experts refer to the "relationship of form to function." What they are saying is that a horse's conformation must enable the horse to engage in the discipline his owner or rider has selected.

You wouldn't want a cutting horse, for example, to be structured like a Thoroughbred, which can run a mile at speed. Nor would you

The horse must be built for the job.

want a five-gaited Saddlebred structured like a stout roping horse.

The form must fit the function intended for the horse. Fortunately for the trail rider, a number of forms can fit the function of trail riding. Trail horses can range from the retired racing Thoroughbred to the former cutting horse. Trail horses can be tall, short, or medium, though length of leg can affect their ability to cover ground. And, as mentioned earlier, they can be of any breed.

While form to function has a good deal of latitude in dealing with trail horses, there's no room for poor conformation. For the purposes of trail riding, I'll define poor conformation as bodily defects that can affect a horse's ability to carry a rider over trails and remain sound while doing so.

A horseman I deeply respected, who also happened to be my father, used to lecture me repeatedly about the importance of sound legs and feet in a horse. "It's just like the foundation of a house," he used to say. "Unless you have a good foundation, that house won't stand, no matter how pretty it might be. If your horse doesn't have good feet and legs, it won't hold up either, no matter how pretty or fancy it is."

It was sound advice then and still is. The horse you choose for your trail-riding companion must, above all else, have sound, solid feet and legs, devoid of deformities that might bring on injury and lameness.

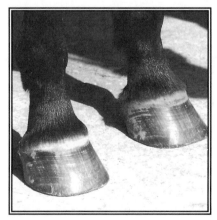
Examine the feet carefully.

From the Ground Up

When you examine a potential trail horse, take a long, hard look at its feet. Are they dry and brittle, with an irregular hoof surface, resulting from pieces being broken off? Do cracks run from the ground to the coronary band? These hooves are telling you that they're going to be trouble from day one. They will wear down rapidly unless the horse is shod, but shoeing may not be the answer either. Brittle hooves don't hold nails well.

You might be able to rehabilitate hooves like these over time, but they don't grow all that rapidly — only about a quarter of an inch per month and even less than that during the winter and in very dry conditions — and the problem will likely resurface.

Watch particularly for quarter cracks — those small breaks in the rear of the hoof that can run from the ground to the coronary band. They're difficult to heal and can cause extreme lameness. Think of a quarter crack in relation to your fingernail. The coronary band corresponds to the cuticle. A split in your fingernail all the way up to the cuticle is extremely painful. It's the same for a horse with a quarter crack that runs into the coronary band.

Be alert also for hooves with odd-looking ridges. When a horse has had a bout with laminitis (founder), the normal smooth-growth pattern is interrupted and the hoof wall often has a ribbed appearance. A single ridge is not much cause for concern. Often horses that experience some trauma or illness, especially with a fever, develop a single ridge on the hoof wall, which disappears when the hoof grows. But multiple ridges are a warning flag. If you see these ridges, have a veterinarian take X-rays before you make the purchase. You need to find out if the interior of the foot has sustained permanent damage.

A good hoof is symmetrical, solid, durable, and devoid of cracks and ridges. For years horsemen argued the merits of black hooves versus white, with the majority thinking black hooves were stronger and more durable. Science has proved that belief to be a fallacy. White hooves are simply an extension of white leg markings. White hair (with underlying pink skin) means the foundation area on the horse lacks pigment, nothing more, just like the white markings on a horse's face. Therefore, a horse with a white pastern will have a white hoof, and a horse with no leg marking will have a black hoof. Some horses have dark stripes on white hooves. In this case you'll find dark hair (often called a "freckle") within that leg marking that touches the hoof. That area on the hoof wall will correspondingly be black. (Don't confuse the striped hooves found on Appaloosas with this common occurrence. The genetics of that breed's hoof wall striping are different and have nothing to do with leg markings.) So, it doesn't matter whether the hoof is white or black; what matters is that it's unblemished and healthy.

Foot size should match the size of the horse. There was a time in the breeding of Quarter Horses and other stock horses shown at halter when it was fashionable to have a huge, barrel-chested horse walking around on tiny feet. To some, this looked good in the show ring, but to the trail rider this type of conformation would be considered defective. Those feet are the horse's foundation for supporting weight, and if the foundation is too small, it will crumble.

Conversely, you don't want a horse with big, flat feet that look like dinner plates. Feet that are too big can be clumsy, just the opposite of a sure-footed animal, and flat feet bruise easily, especially on rocky terrain. Look for feet that are in balance with the horse's body size, have a somewhat concave sole, and appear solid and symmetrical.

Sound Legs

While the feet are the underpinning of a horse's "foundation," the legs carry the weight and provide propulsion so the horse can cover ground. Strong, healthy, properly conformed legs are a must in the trail horse.

No feet, no horse. No legs, no horse.

When it comes to a horse's limbs, it's indisputable that conformation is a major factor in soundness. And, there can be little argument that the degree of soundness affects the immediate usefulness of the horse as well as its longevity as a trail mount. Though other problems can befall trail horses, my guess is that the vast majority become unfit for riding because of lameness problems.

Granted, trail riding does not put the same stresses on a horse's limbs as jumping, cutting, or racing, but when a horse is carrying a rider over rugged terrain, even at a walk, every step brings stresses and pressures. Only properly conformed legs hold up for season after season of trail riding.

Part of the difficulty in finding a trail horse prospect with good leg conformation can be blamed on man. Before man became heavily involved with the horse, nature did an excellent job of culling on the basis of leg conformation. The horse that was lame and couldn't flee predators became their next meal. Nature and necessity judged proper conformation. Today, man has put himself in that role. Rarely, except in certain wild bands, do nature and necessity still figure into the equation.

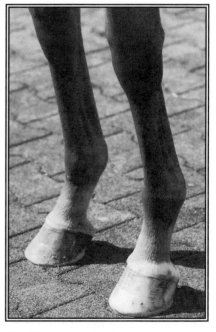

Good legs are a must.

The problem with man's involvement is his decisions are based on opinion influenced by the fashion of the moment along with economic factors, rather than what is best for the breed.

Take a look at Thoroughbred racing. What happens when a top runner breaks down? It goes immediately into a breeding program so that it can produce other horses that will also break down when subjected to the same stresses.

The same is true of show-ring fashion. I've already mentioned the tiny feet once in vogue for Quarter Horses and other stock horses shown at halter. If one of these horses, with its manicured, tiny hooves supporting a huge body, were turned loose with a wild band in a harsh environment, it would soon become so lame it would perish.

In breeds where a gaited championship is the goal, proper leg conformation might be sacrificed if the horse being bred has the potential to trot and rack on with class, style, and animation. The horse may not be long for the performance world, but while it's there, it may perform brilliantly with legs that will be able to take only so much pounding. It's then placed in a breeding program that produces more horses with malformed legs.

In considering a potential trail horse, you should look through the eyes of nature when judging whether the animal has proper leg conformation. If you proceed on the assumption that this horse will have to fend for itself in a harsh environment that includes hard, rocky ground, you'll not lead yourself astray. You'll quickly turn away from anything that doesn't have hardy hooves and strong, sound legs.

The Front End

The front legs are of utmost importance in your trail-riding horse because they carry between 60 percent and 65 percent of the animal's weight. There are no bony attachments between a horse's front legs and the rest of its skeleton. The attachment is via muscles and tendons. In the human body there is bony attachment between the trunk of the body and arms and legs through the shoulder blades. With the horse it's as though the front part of the body is suspended in a sling formed by the two front legs.

In addition to supporting most of the animal's weight, the front legs also serve as shock absorbers, dissipating the concussion that comes with each stride.

When you look at your potential trail horse from the side, you want to see a well-angled shoulder. The degree of angle will vary, but it must give the appearance of a shoulder that is laid back as opposed to straight up and down. If you detect very little angle to the shoulder, be ready to move on, because you're looking at a horse that will have a short, choppy stride, along with future leg problems.

Why? The bone responsible for the angle is the shoulder bone or scapula. Attached to it is the humerus. It angles back from the chest to a point where it connects with the forearm or radius, which travels downward to the knee. Take a look at the diagram of a horse's skeleton and you'll see instantly what I'm talking about. The diagram shows a horse with good conformation. Because the shoulder blades are properly angled, the horse has the ability to stride out freely and absorb shock well.

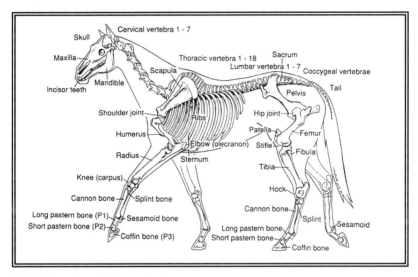

Skeletal system of the entire horse.

Now, mentally remove that angle and imagine a conformation with a straight shoulder. Immediately the horse's ability to stride out disappears, as does the shock-absorbing capability, because the angle of the pastern, that part of the limb between the ankle and hoof, generally follows that of the shoulder. The pastern is designed to flex as the foot strikes the ground, thus helping to absorb shock. When the pastern is short and straight, the horse has a short, jolting stride that may quickly compromise its soundness. Because the short-strided horse's feet will hit the ground more frequently over a given distance, each footfall will solidly jolt bones, ligaments, and tendons, and be uncomfortable for the rider.

Still standing at the side of the horse, look down the leg from the knee to the pastern. This is the cannon bone. If you happen to be in the company of an old-time horseman, he might tell you to look for a leg with "flat bone." There is not a bone in the horse's leg that is flat. The reference is to a large, round cannon bone equipped with a suspensory ligament, a deep flexor tendon, and a superficial flexor tendon large enough to match the size of the bone. When viewed from the side, the leg structure appears flat. The large bone and correspondingly large tendons and ligaments translate into a strong leg.

To check for good conformation in the front legs, look for a leg that's straight from the top of the forearm to the fetlock, with the angle of the pastern into the hoof at about the same degree as the angle of the shoulder.

Make sure you check whether a horse is back at the knee or calf-kneed, the most serious front-end conformational fault. The condition results from a posterior or rearward deviation of the knee joint. This deviation puts undue stress on the horse's ligaments and tendons with each step. Those ligaments and tendons function properly only when the knee joint is correctly aligned. This type of leg conformation is definitely not what nature would choose. A bone column that's bent backward puts heavy stress on the entire tendon, muscle, ligament, and joint structure.

The opposite of calf-kneed is over at the knee or buck kneed, also a conformational defect. While neither defect is desirable, the calf-kneed horse is by far more risky. The horse that is over at the knee at least has the defect in the direction the knee normally bends.

Now step in front of the horse and look at those same legs from this vantage point. To check for straightness in each of the limbs, drop an imaginary plumb line from the top of the forearm down the leg. A vertical line should run through the middle of the knee, cannon bone, pastern, and hoof.

If one or both of the front hooves turn out (toeing out), this is a serious conformational fault because each stride will put a great deal of pressure on the inside of the knee. Unfortunately, that isn't all. When this horse travels, it will wing in with each stride and be in danger of striking the coronary band, sesamoids, and splint bones. A horse that toes out severely is a poor candidate for a trail horse.

A horse can also toe in, called pigeon-toed, a less serious conformational defect, and one that causes fewer lameness problems. The pigeon-toed horse paddles or swings its feet out when traveling, and while this type of conformation places unnatural stress on joints, ligaments, and tendons, the horse, at least, doesn't strike itself.

From the hooves, let your eyes travel up to the horse's pasterns. At one time, a popular theory (which you'll read in many older texts) was that the front pasterns should form a forty-five-degree angle. That is no longer believed to be the case, with the angle varying from horse to horse. A fifty-two- to fifty-five-degree angle is much more realistic and common among all breeds of horses. But the most important thing is that the angle of the pastern is the same as the angle of the hoof. The proper alignment enhances soundness because the underlying structures are not under stress. A horse with a pastern angle that doesn't match the hoof (a broken axis) will have a hard time staying sound.

When picking a trail-riding horse, also make sure the slope of the pastern is not excessive — coon-footed. This conformational fault indicates weak pasterns that will not hold up under even moderate use. Conversely, if the horse has pasterns that look like vertical posts, you're going to be dealing with a mount that has a short, choppy stride with little or no shock-absorbing capability — this would be the horse with the straight shoulder.

Hind Legs

To check the hind legs, view them first from the side. You're looking for a leg that's not excessively straight and not excessively angled. You'd want to see the imaginary plumb line travel down the rear leg from the back of the buttocks to the point of the hock, down to the fetlock, then straight to the ground, landing about three inches behind the foot.

A rear leg with too much angle is referred to as sickle-hocked. Whether climbing hills and mountains or even traveling across flat land, a horse with sickle hocks strains the ligaments running over the hocks because they are designed for a more direct pathway down the leg, rather than being angled forward.

If, on the other hand, the leg is too straight, called "post-legged" or "straight behind," there can also be problems with getting a smooth ride and the horse remaining sound. Viewed from the side, this leg will have very little angle between tibia and femur, and the hock will appear straight. This condition increases tension on the hock joint

capsule, causing irritation and distention. The horse will not be able to stride out properly with its rear leg and will have a choppy gait. Also, because the animal's weight is not supported properly, the horse is out of balance and can become lame.

An exaggeration of this condition occurs when the rear legs are placed too far rearward. The horse is described

View the horse from behind.

as "camped out." This condition results in similar strain on the hock as in the horse that is straight behind. A horse so afflicted will also have trouble "getting under himself" with those rear legs for traction or braking.

Next view the horse from behind. From this vantage point you want to see legs that are straight. A horse that toes out behind, with its hocks close together, is "cow-hocked." If the fault is severe, the horse will stress its hocks, as well as its stifles.

The horse that has the opposite problem — hocks too wide apart — puts even more unnatural strain on hocks and stifles and has trouble traveling correctly. A horse with this type of problem is rarely a good athlete for any endeavor and definitely a poor candidate as a trail horse.

The slope of the rear pasterns should also match the slope of the hoof, though the rear angle of the pasterns is normally steeper.

The Whole Horse

After you've assessed all four legs, look at the horse in its entirety. The key word here is "balance." You don't want massive shoulders and a tiny rear end or vice versa. As your eyes travel over the horse's body, there should be a smooth melding of parts from attractive head, to long neck, to prominent withers, to strong back and loin on through the hips and along the croup to the tail.

Start with the head. You want a head that's pleasing to look at with large eyes set on the corners of the forehead and large nostrils. The face should be straight or slightly dished. You do not want a bulging, "Roman nosed" face with small, narrow eyes.

Proper head configuration is important for several reasons. First, you want the eyes wide-set to give the horse better range of vision. (See Chapter 3.) When the eyes are properly set, the horse has almost 360-degree vision. The horse with small eyes and a Roman nose has trouble seeing properly because the bulge of the nasal bone obstructs the horse's vision. When a horse can't see well, it can be flighty, cantankerous, and even mean.

There's also a reason for large nostrils. A horse can't breathe through its mouth, so the entire oxygen supply for that large body must be inhaled through the nostrils. If they are narrow and constricted, the horse can't get enough air when stressed on a trail ride.

A coarse, heavy jowl could indicate insufficient room for the pharynx and esophagus. A horse that is wide between the jaws is one that will have plenty of room for air and food passageways. Everything that makes it possible for that horse to live and perform must go through the throatlatch — air, food, its total nerve supply, and blood to and from the brain. The horse with a heavy jowl and thick throatlatch will have serious problems when you ask it to tuck its head (give to the bit) and go to work. Sort of like buttoning at the neck a shirt that's one size too small, a horse with a thick throatlatch will have trouble breathing and swallowing.

The ideal trail horse should have a moderately long neck. The horse uses its neck as a balancing arm for its body mass. This really becomes obvious when you watch a cutting horse in action. These horses must stop and change directions in a flash to follow and control the movements of the calf in front of them. A long, flexible neck assists in maintaining balance. A horse with a short, thick neck just simply can't maintain balance as well. Trail horses also use their necks as balancers when climbing or descending a hill. The climbing horse lowers its neck, freeing up the hindquarters to reach forward and dig in for more traction. The horse descending a hill will tend to raise its neck, shifting more of its weight to the rear quarters.

Good withers and a strong back are important.

A good trail horse should have prominent withers for a basic reason — to keep the saddle in place. A horse with low or round withers — "mutton withered" — will need a mighty-tight cinch to keep the saddle in proper position. And when you draw the cinch too tightly, you're compromising your horse's ability to breathe, plus making him darned uncomfortable.

You want a horse with a straight back, not a swayed or arched one. A back that isn't straight won't allow the saddle to rest properly, possibly creating muscle pain and saddle sores. The saddle should rest on the muscles running on either side of the spine. This is not possible with an arched or a swayed back.

The back should be of moderate length, neither too short nor too long. There's no magic length for a horse's back, but it should have sufficient room for your saddle.

A back that's too long tends to be weak, and in time, your weight and that of the saddle could cause your horse to become sore.

It's rare to find a horse with an excessively short back. On such a horse, make sure your saddle is not so long as to rub into the horse's croup area. That will cause him a lot of discomfort and rub sores.

Some Arabians have rather short backs because they have one less vertebra in their spinal column. Some saddles are specifically made with Arabian-type trees to accommodate the breed's typical conformation. The tree is the foundation on which the saddle is constructed. I strongly suggest if you ride a short-backed Arabian that you purchase a saddle to fit the horse properly.

The back should have good muscling over the loin area. The horse's muscles have to tense the whole spinal column so that it can operate the front end with all its weight, plus that of its rider.

The Croup

While it is a given that the croup, that part of the topline from the tailhead to the top of the hip, should be long so that the horse is capable of a lengthy stride behind, there's no universal slope that is perfect. Generally speaking, for example, Arabians have flatter croups than Quarter Horses. The slope to the croup is determined by the way in which the horse's pelvis is attached to its body and that determines the length of stride of the back leg. What you should be looking for in your trail horse is an animal that has a long, moderately sloped croup. A short croup usually means that the horse has a long back that will be lacking in strength. Length of croup is measured from the tailhead to the highest point at the top of the hip. This indicates the point at which the ilium, the largest of three bones in the pelvis, connects with the spinal column.

A horse's croup can be too level and that's as much of a detriment as being too sloped. A case in point: An Arabian mare that my wife Linda used to ride has a very level croup. She has a good, long stride and is comfortable to ride but has trouble getting her legs beneath her descending steep ground.

We were riding in Bridger-Teton National Forest and came to an extremely steep descent with no switchbacks; it was pretty much a solid, rocky surface. I started down with my Thoroughbred gelding, leading three pack mules. We descended slowly and carefully without a problem, each animal using powerful rear legs as brakes.

Linda started down after me and was in immediate trouble. The flat-crouped mare was unable to get her rear legs into proper braking position and began skidding down the steep slope. I stopped my horse and the pack string to use them as barriers. Her mare skidded into the rear mule, pushing it into the next one and that mule continued the chain reaction by being forced into the lead mule. He was a powerful brute and simply stood his ground, bringing everyone to a halt.

A shaken Linda dismounted and walked the rest of the way down, her mare slipping and sliding beside her. The mare has since been retired from serious mountain riding.

That experience proves the point that you want your trail horse to have a long stride to cover ground but also enough power to get you up steep slopes and to maintain balance coming back down; in other words, a horse with a moderately sloped croup.

The Horse's Barrel

Finally, look at the horse's barrel, that part of the body that houses heart, lungs, liver, and stomach. You want to see a reasonable spring of rib (bowed or rounded as opposed to flat-sided) so these organs have plenty of room to function properly without being constricted.

However, a horse with an overly round barrel will be hard to ride since your legs will constantly be bowed. That really hurts over the miles — your knees especially will be sore. When you take the prospective trail horse on a test ride, pay attention to where your legs hang. You want them straight down for maximum comfort. If they're flared out at all, you'll experience pain before too long. And no trail ride is fun when your body is hurting.

6

TRAIL 101
Training and Conditioning the Novice Trail Horse

It's beyond the scope of this book to get too detailed in the training and conditioning of horses, but in this chapter I will concentrate on the basics for any good trail horse. (I'm going to assume that your horse has a good disposition and sound conformation and has already been trained or broke to ride but lacks experience on the trail.)

There are as many theories about training horses as there are trainers. Hundreds of articles and books have been written about the "correct" way to start and finish a horse for a number of disciplines. I have read many of them and have observed some top trainers in action. My conclusion is you can follow one of many basic approaches, but no single method guarantees success because horses are individuals and must be treated as such.

Pressure and Release

If there's one single method that comes close to encompassing what training a horse is all about, it's pressure and release. It's a training philosophy as well as a technique, used by many top trainers today. The simplest way to explain it is this: You apply pressure on a horse to do something, and the instant he does it you release the pressure. In other words, the horse moves away from the pressure, and his reward is that he isn't pressured anymore.

For example, to get a horse to move forward, squeeze his sides with your legs. When he moves forward (away from pressure), stop squeezing. Combine a squeeze from the legs with pressure on the bit and the horse should move backward. The "pressure" list goes on, no matter what the discipline — from dressage to trail riding.

Through pressure and release techniques, a common theme throughout this chapter, you can control every part of your horse's body and, therefore, navigate him around, through, and over any kind of terrain.

The Basics

Several basics are a must for your trail horse; in fact, they're requirements for any well-trained horse.

First, your horse must lead properly. You should be able to lead him, from the side or from the front, without trying to run over you or pull away. There may be times on the trail when you must lead him through a narrow space. You'll need a horse that will follow

A horse should lead willingly.

readily but not walk on your heels. The horse must respect your space and not invade it.

Here is a simple technique that can help the horse understand about space. Using a lead shank that is eight to ten feet long, step in front of your horse while leading it. Walk backward while facing the horse. Give a verbal command to "Whoa." Simultaneously flick the lead shank with an up-and-down motion so that the section near the halter flips against the horse's chin. In the beginning it may take multiple flips before the horse stops. Combine each flip with the command "Whoa," but keep moving backward so that the horse doesn't close the space between the two of you. Stop when the horse stops. Repeat the exercise until the horse stops on the verbal command only.

Now, carry the exercise one step further. Step toward the horse with the verbal command to back. Simultaneously twirl the lead rope in a rolling motion that will again bring it into contact with the jaw area. Very soon the horse will be backing as a result of the lead rope flicks, your verbal command, and your approach. Notice that the flicks are administered differently — up and down to halt the horse and circularly to convince it to move back. This difference will avoid confusing the horse as to what you are asking.

The important thing is that these two simple exercises will teach the horse always to yield space to you.

At the same time, you are teaching responses to verbal commands. "Whoa" must mean stop, for instance. It also helps to have a horse that can be soothed by a low-pitched, calm voice in an excitable situation.

Still other important basics for your horse include being easy to saddle and bridle and standing still when tied and for mounting. Here are some tips for accomplishing those tasks.

Saddling

Saddling should be a calm, gradual affair for horses at all levels of training, not a sudden burst of action. To begin, fold the off stirrup and both front and back cinches over the seat of the saddle. Then, from the left side, lift and place the saddle quietly and gently on the horse's back. Walk around to the other side, and, just as gently and quietly, lower the stirrup and cinches. Back to the left side, take up the cinch with a light first pull. When the horse relaxes, tighten the cinch a bit more. You may have to do this two or three times, but it will give the horse time to relax and exhale, turning a potentially painful experience into one that's not in the least bit traumatic.

If the horse continues to fidget and step about even though you're quiet and calm in your saddling approach, it's time to place the animal in a position where fidgeting is not possible. The corner of a square corral works well. In front will be one barrier of the corral and on the horse's right side will be another. You can tie the horse to

Standing quietly while being saddled.

the corral fence in front so that the animal can't back away. Thus, you have four barriers — the fence in front, the fence to the right, the lead rope that prevents movement to the rear, and your presence on the left.

Place the saddle quietly on the horse's back. Don't draw up the cinch. Remove the saddle and put it back on. Do this over and over until your horse becomes desensitized and learns it's no big deal to have the saddle on his back. Standing still should then come easily. When your horse allows you to saddle him without moving about, remove the restraining obstacles. Eventually, you won't need the fence in front or to the right, and tying the horse at all soon should be unnecessary.

One thing that definitely won't work is abuse. If you slap or whip the horse that fidgets, you're only going to make the problem worse.

Bridling

Once the horse is saddled, it's time for bridling. If your horse has a tendency to raise his head anytime you do something to his mouth, spend some time working with the poll (that area between the ears) to overcome the problem. The poll is very sensitive, and if you exert gentle pressure with thumb and forefinger, the horse should lower his head to move away from pressure. The moment he drops his head, release all pressure. Soon, the mere presence of your arm over the poll will cause the horse to lower his head to the bit automatically.

Because your horse has been conditioned to lower his head from pressure on the poll, you should make use of that when bridling. Grip the top of the headstall with your right hand and extend your right arm over the horse's head so that it rests between the ears. Cradle the bit in your left hand. Gently pull the bridle upward with your right arm. If the horse does not open his mouth for the bit, use your left thumb to exert pressure on the bars — that toothless area between incisors and molars — while continuing to hold the bit in your left palm. Normally, this is all that is required, and the horse will open his mouth in response to pressure.

Once the bit is in place, switch hands by gripping the top of the headstall with your left hand. Use your right hand to fold the right ear inward very gently, and push it slightly forward while sliding the headstall over it. Do the same with the left ear, and you will have executed a trauma-free bridling.

Many bridling problems originate in bridle removal. This should be done very gently. With your left hand at the bit, gently slip the headstall forward over the ears with your right hand. As you lower it, use your left hand on the bit to ease it out of the mouth without banging it against the horse's teeth.

Standing Still Tied

The horse that won't stand still while tied or being saddled is very disconcerting. Novice horses aren't the only ones with this bad habit; **This horse stands still while tied.**

even well-broke horses are culprits. They must have missed this very important lesson in the beginning of their training.

With any of his young horses, my friend Jim McCray employs a procedure he calls "soaking." He ties the horse to a safe board fence or hitch rack with two lead ropes snapped onto the halter — one extending to the left and the other to the right — to prevent the horse from twisting and turning. The horse can move about a bit but is at least partially restricted. The horse stands there, for hours if need be, and learns that fidgeting accomplishes nothing. Some horses require several soaking sessions to teach them that it's much easier to stand quietly while tied than to be constantly moving about.

Once the horse learns to stand quietly for what you consider to be a satisfactory period, you should reward him by returning him to his stall or paddock. The acceptable amount of time to leave him tied will vary. In the beginning it may be only for a few minutes. As the horse progresses, you might want him to remain tied for an hour or two. Your goal is to reach a point where the horse will stand quietly if tied to a trailer all night.

The soaking sessions are also beneficial to the horse that doesn't want to stand while being saddled. Of course, you should remember that a part of this problem might be your fault if you simply slap on the saddle, grab the cinch strap, and haul 'er up tight. Your poor horse is standing quietly one moment, and in the next he's having a heavy object unceremoniously slammed onto his back and a cinch drawn up tight as a bow string. It's no wonder some horses won't stand still when being saddled.

Mounting

Your horse should stand still for being mounted as well. Having him move off while you're attempting to mount is unacceptable. If you have saddlebags and a bedroll to swing your leg over, this bad habit can be frustrating and even dangerous.

To break the horse of this habit, start at ground level. When you prepare to mount, have the reins ready in your left hand. Put your foot in the stirrup and pause. If your horse even hints at moving forward, check (rein) him up. When he's standing quietly, swing up, but don't completely mount. Stop, standing upright in the left stirrup. (Make certain that the cinch is tightened so the saddle doesn't slip.) If the horse tries to move off, check him up again. If he starts spinning around, don't put yourself in jeop-

The horse should remain still.

ardy by remaining standing in the stirrup. Step down, make the horse stand quietly for a time, and then start over. When your horse stands without moving while you balance in the left stirrup, swing the rest of the way into the saddle.

If the horse moves off in this final phase of the mounting process, bring him immediately to a stop and back him five or six steps. Then stop again and make him stand quietly. Dismount and repeat the process.

To reinforce to your horse that he must stand still for being mounted, always require him to remain still for a short time after being mounted.

It will take several lessons if your horse is confirmed in this bad habit, but you can break him of it if you're relentless in never letting him get away with doing so, even when you might be in a hurry.

Common Fears

Before you ever set foot on a trail, you can do several things at home to prepare your horse for what he'll encounter, including finding out what scares him and helping him overcome his fears.

It's a good idea to determine what scares your horse before he has to face "monsters" on the trail. If you perform the following series of tests, you can see right in your own front yard how your horse will react to certain obstacles and distractions.

For example, to see if your horse is scared of objects blowing in the wind, have someone swing a large piece of plastic or a rain-slicker in his vicinity. Performing this test from the ground with you holding the reins or lead rope might save you from getting dumped if the horse becomes badly frightened. It's normal for horses to become exceedingly alert when around fluttering objects, and you don't want a trail horse that panics.

To find out your horse's tolerance for dogs, ride him around the yard while your dog (or a friend's if you don't have one) is bounding about. You want the horse aware of the dog and its movements but not frightened.

Is the horse afraid of strange, stationary objects? Ride him up to whatever happens to be in your yard — parked machinery, a bicycle, garbage can, whatever.

Is your horse afraid of motor vehicles? To find out, start up the noisiest vehicle you have — diesel truck, tractor, whatever — and have someone rev up the engine while you ride the horse back and forth past it. The loud noise of an engine is an assault on a horse's keen sense of hearing, but you don't want your horse to turn and run from the vehicle.

Motorcycles can be extremely frightening to horses. It may have something to do with their difficulty in focusing on a narrow object that's moving toward them at speed. If you don't have a motorcycle, find someone who does and ask your friend to come over and ride it in your driveway while you hold your horse. Again, it's normal for the horse to be somewhat apprehensive in the presence of a motorcycle, but you don't want panic.

Close Call

Trail horses that are afraid of cars, motorcycles, and other moving equipment can be a danger to themselves and their riders. I remember a strapping young Appaloosa gelding I was training as a trail horse some years back. The horse seemed calm and tractable enough around the stable and in the training corral, but I had not put him through the tests mentioned above.

Instead, I simply rode him down the driveway and onto a gravel road. We were doing fine until a car came up behind us. I moved the horse to the opposite side of the road and was turning him to face the oncoming vehicle so that he could see what was approaching, when, without warning, he leaped right into the path of the car. Fortunately for all concerned, the driver had slowed down when he saw me on the road — folks in the area were used to seeing me riding there — and was able to stop quickly. The experience shook both horse and humans; it was a lesson learned.

Know your horse's fears and overcome them before exposing the animal to dangerous challenges on the trail.

Innate Fear of Water

One thing seems to be a given with nearly all horses unless they were born and raised on open range or in pastures with creeks and

Accustoming a horse to water with the help of a lead horse.

ponds — they have an innate fear of water. (See Chapter 2.) It all has to do with their survival instincts. You should expect this fear in your new trail horse and take steps to conquer it. If he isn't afraid of water, you're one step ahead of the game, and your new horse is one step closer to being a good trail mount.

You can begin in the horse's paddock or pasture. To find out if the horse is afraid of water, let the water tank overflow and watch his reaction when he approaches the tank for a drink. Does he notice the water but walk to the tank without hesitating? If so, he has passed the first test. If, however, he snorts and sniffs at the water in fear, you might be facing a problem on the trail when you come to a stream or mud puddle. If the horse is fearful of water, make sure he has daily contact with it, such as keeping water standing around the tank.

Desensitization

If your horse fails to pass any of these "fear" tests, then desensitize him. Accomplish this with repetition — exposing the animal over and over to whatever is causing fear. How you handle the horse at this time is very important. You want to be quiet, confident, and firm. If your

horse is fearful of something, reassure him with your voice and relaxed attitude. If you act nonchalant, the horse might very well take his cues from you and walk by the object or through the obstacle without hesitation, your ultimate goal.

You shouldn't force your horse to confront the object by using your spurs strongly.

An old fear becomes a new friend.

Your horse might associate pain from the excessive spurring with the scary object. You'll confirm his fear or suspicion of the object, and you'll have accomplished exactly the opposite of what you wanted.

Instead, apply slight pressure with a squeeze from your legs or just a light touch of the spurs to send the message that the horse must move forward. The second he offers even one tiny step, release the pressure and praise him profusely with kind words and soothing rubs. He'll know that he's done well and that nothing hurt him when he moved toward the scary object.

Walk or Jump Over Obstacles

When trail riding, you will often encounter obstacles that must be stepped over, such as logs. You may even be faced with an obstacle that must be jumped. Again, you can begin a trail-training program in your own front yard. Start by putting three or more wooden poles on the ground about three to four feet apart.

Ride the horse over them at a walk, letting him drop his nose to sniff at them if he wishes. In the beginning your horse may appear to have poor timing or coordination with his feet, touching or stepping on the poles as he crosses them. Soon, however, the horse should pick his way through the poles — whether he's walking or trotting — without touching them, no matter how close together you place them.

When you reach this point, it's time to challenge your horse a bit more. Elevate one of the poles eight to twelve inches off the ground and ask

Negotiating an obstacle.

the horse to step over it. He may strike the pole with a foot a few times, but soon he'll step over with care.

Now it's time to speed up the pace. Try taking the obstacle at a trot. If the horse simply trots over the obstacle, that's okay, but your ultimate goal is to get him to jump it. To help the horse visualize what's in front of him, place another pole on the ground about two feet in front of the raised pole. This will help him establish a takeoff point.

Your goal here is to have a trail horse that will quietly step over obstacles or jump them if need be. Here's a word of warning. When you do get on the trail, you must know what's on the other side of a downed tree or obstacle before you ask your horse to jump it. You don't want him sailing over a downed tree and landing in a hole. You must also remember that you're dealing with a trail horse and not an arena jumper. If the obstacle appears too high to jump safely, find a way around it. Leaving the prescribed trail and picking your way through brush and timber, known as brush popping, is good practice for any trail horse. Do make certain, however, that you are not riding where leaving the trail is prohibited.

Downed Timber

Downed timber is common on trails all over this country and is one of the prime reasons for teaching your horse to go over obstacles when called upon. An overnight storm can send trees crashing down on a trail that you might be taking the next day.

An obvious option is to let an experienced horse lead the way. Normally, confidence comes quickly once your horse realizes that the horse he's following had no problem stepping over the downed log.

But if you don't have someone to follow, your training at home over the poles will come in handy. Ride your horse up to the fallen log or tree and allow him to inspect it closely. Let him get a good look at it, even smell it. This will also allow you an opportunity to examine what is on the other side. Then gently persuade him with your legs and spurs (lightly, no jabbing) to cross. The moment he lifts a leg to get over the log, cease with your pressure. That's your horse's reward for doing well, and he understands it. Pressure and release. Throughout the whole scenario try to let him figure out the obstacle at his own pace. Now is not the time to rush him. Give him time to think it out. Having patience on your early training rides will pay off with big dividends down the road.

Negotiating obstacles can be fun.

Once your horse gets across, even if he's clumsy, praise him heartily for a job well done. He'll know he did what you wanted, and his confidence will grow. He'll begin to think that there's nothing that you ask that he can't do.

If the timber is too high to step over easily, you may have to jump. Again, follow the routine you used at home. Allow the horse to look over the timber; then turn around and retrace your steps to have enough room to jump. Try approaching the timber at a trot or slow lope. Your horse may leap high the first time or two, so grab your saddle horn and hold on. Once over, let your horse know how happy you are with him. Over time he'll be less apt to pop over the downed timber and, instead, will jump with quiet confidence.

If the timber is too big to step over or jump, you may be faced with finding a path around it in terrain that's steep, thick, and/or rocky. This is not a place where you want a horse to panic because he's never before been asked to leave the trail and work his way around an obstacle.

But as I mentioned previously, it will be helpful if, on earlier training rides, you ask your horse to go off-trail. During practice brush popping, your horse will find the courage and confidence to push his way through thick brush that makes seeing where he's going difficult. This is asking a lot of a green trail horse; but you'll find plenty of times when it's necessary, so explore off-trail to your heart's content where possible.

A calm, steady but firm approach will have an inexperienced horse leading the way over all kinds of obstacles in a short time. The key is to take your time. You don't need, nor should you want, a "thirty-day wonder." It takes years of riding to develop a confident, dependable trail horse, so why be in such an all-fired hurry with the foundation process? If you approach with no timetable, you will enjoy the training program and so will your horse.

Slicker Training

Bad weather, such as rainstorms, is a fact of life on the trail, and you want your horse to be accustomed to a slicker or raincoat before you head out for a ride. Early on you should desensitize your horse to flapping objects, such as slickers being on his back. But start from the ground first. Let the horse sniff the slicker while you stand at the side of his head. Then, shake it out and rub it all over the animal's body, just like you're sacking him out. Flap it over his back, under his belly, and around his legs.

When the horse is completely familiar with this activity, it's time to saddle up and climb aboard. If the horse tends to shy away from strange things, even though he has accepted the raincoat at ground level, it's best to carry out this step in the confines of a corral or round pen.

Once mounted, rub the raincoat over the horse's withers and neck. Then switch to the rump, all the while letting the horse know by talking to him in a low, gentle, and reassuring voice that he won't be harmed. When your horse accepts this, it's time to put on the raincoat. Be sure to keep one hand on the reins, just in case he spooks.

Continue putting on and taking off the raincoat or slicker until the horse is completely desensitized. Do this every day for a week, and you will have a horse that will stand quietly through the whole procedure. You will discover during a sudden rainstorm that this is a mighty fine attribute. If you're forced to dismount to don the raincoat, you might remount to find a soaking wet saddle seat.

Preventing Bad Habits

It's almost as important to prevent the trail horse from learning bad habits as it is to teach him what to do. Bad habits can be annoying to the point that they will totally destroy the fun of a trail ride.

One bad habit that seems benign in the beginning can turn into a downright nuisance — nibbling at grass or leaves while traveling down a trail. If you never let your

A slicker-trained horse.

horse do this, he'll get to the point where he won't even try. However, just lower your guard a little bit and let him drop his head to grab a mouthful of grass a time or two and it'll quickly become a habit. I had one mare that I couldn't break from doing this when she was being ponied as a pack horse.

In dealing with this problem, anticipation is the key. You can sense when your horse is about to make his move at a tuft of grass or a leafy branch. Don't jerk the horse, but do something immediately to change his mind. Check him up lightly to slow the pace, turn his head, or squeeze his sides with your legs to increase the pace. If the horse is successful in getting a tuft of grass or mouthful of leaves, a reprimand will do no good. The horse has already won the battle. Anticipation and quick action are crucial to success.

When stopping for a rest break, always dismount before allowing the horse to graze. The goal should be never to let the horse associate eating with traveling down a trail.

Dawdling is another bad habit. Some horses are lazy by nature and get even lazier with continued riding. Always make certain that your horse is moving at the pace you desire rather than at the pace he wants. Use leg pressure, a tap of the reins, heels, or spurs to convince the horse that he must keep up the pace you want. This trait is especially important when you are riding in a group.

7

TRAINING ON THE TRAIL

Once you've completed your preparatory work at home, you're ready to take your horse on a trail ride. You should pick an easy route for the first ride — one with no serious challenges. And, even better, you should ride with someone aboard an experienced trail horse.

Position in a Group

On your first ride, if possible, start by letting your horse follow the experienced horse. Does your horse walk along quietly with at least

Novices should follow experienced horses and riders.

a horse length between him and the horse in front, or does he want to tailgate the lead horse without watching where he places his feet? You want a horse that is comfortable anywhere in a group, but you don't want him walking with his nose on another horse's rump. If you have a tailgater, you'll want to check him up quietly anytime he comes within less than a horse length to the horse in front of him.

Find out next what happens when you're the leader. When you put the horse up front for the first time, make sure you know the trail and are certain that no scary obstacles are ahead. By keeping the ride free of challenges the first few times, you can get a better idea of how he'll react to being the lead horse in a group. Encountering scary obstacles while in the lead should come later.

Teaching a horse to take the lead.

Your hope and goal should be that your new trail horse will walk along with confidence while, at the same time, being fully aware of all that's going on around him.

It's a good idea, if possible, to have at least two other companions on the first ride. Then, you'll be able to put the horse between two others and check his reaction when there's a horse in front and one behind him. Some horses don't mind following but become nervous when a horse is behind them.

If your horse is apprehensive about having another horse and rider behind him, you should desensitize your horse to that situation. The rider following you should be mounted on a calm, steady horse. Ask your companion to close the gap between horses slowly. Have the trailing rider move up fairly close, but not too close, being aware that your horse might become frightened and kick. Then ask your friend to ride alongside your horse, first on the left and then on the right. The aim is for your horse to realize that there's nothing to fear from having a horse behind or beside him.

Your goal on an initial trail ride should be a highly pleasurable experience for the horse with a lot of walking and trotting along established trails in the company of calm, well-mannered equine companions. You may, perhaps, include an excursion or two off the trail into some brush to make sure the horse looks where he places his feet.

Of course, riding with companions is not always possible. If you are taking that first trail ride solo, you should exude patience and calmness. The horse will depend on you for his security. If you are calm and quiet, you communicate that all is well and he has nothing to fear.

Crossing Water

After a few uneventful rides, seek more challenging trips, such as crossing mud puddles or shallow streams. Because horses will always go around rather than through water, pick the spot for this lesson with care. Don't ask the horse to go through a mud puddle, for instance, when dry ground is on both sides. Instead, find a place where there's no alternative but to cross at the spot you've chosen. Your horse may still not want to cross, but no other options will be available.

I remember watching, perplexed, when one of the riders on a trail ride decided she would teach her horse to go through a water puddle that the horse was avoiding. The only problem was that the puddle was in the center of the trail with firm, dry ground on both sides. The woman became exasperated and then angry when the horse refused the water route and opted for dry land.

She didn't realize that the horse was following age-old instincts. Why should it go through water when a dry route was available? The supposed lesson ended with the horse never setting foot in the water and the woman finishing the ride still frustrated and angry.

When you approach water for the first time, you want the horse to

This horse balks when he sees water.

realize that no other options exist other than going through the water. A shallow stream where the horse can see the bottom works best for a first-time crossing water.

With our method, Linda leads the way on her gelding, with me right behind on the inexperienced trail horse. If the new horse is nervous and apprehensive, Linda might ride her gelding into the stream and stop him. I bring the novice horse up behind and let him look at the water and realize that Linda's horse isn't the least bit worried. Then, Linda will ride across the stream, and I will urge my horse to follow. Sometimes novice horses follow immediately.

The objective at this point is not only that you succeed in what you set out to do, no matter how long it takes, but also that you accomplish your goal without using undue force. Never start one of these sessions unless you have all the time in the world to complete it.

But the rider firmly urges him on...

In the above case, if my horse is overly fearful, I might mount Linda's horse and lead the inexperienced animal. While aboard her gelding, I'll attempt to pressure the horse into the water, with the veteran gelding serving two purposes — providing the pressure via the lead rope and continuing to serve as a security blanket. Normally, this method works, and the horse yields to the lead-rope pressure. Sometimes Linda and I combine pressures, with me applying pressure on the halter from the saddle of the veteran and Linda, on the ground, gently tapping the youngster from the rear with a longe whip.

Again, you might not have the luxury of being accompanied by someone on a veteran horse when you come to water. If that is the case, you should

...then rewards the horse.

carefully pick and choose the point of the water-crossing lesson. The best spot would be a broad trail, free of rocks and obstacles, crossing a clear stream with a firm bottom. As mentioned earlier, the first water-crossing lesson on the trail should be preceded by lessons at home.

When you are riding alone and encounter a water crossing, ride right up to it without hesitation, thus communicating to the horse that this is just another part of the trail. However, if the horse wants to stop and check things out, don't force him to go forward until he has satisfied his curiosity. Let him lower his head and sniff the water. Give him time to learn that no monsters lurk within and then squeeze with your legs to urge him forward, talking to him softly and reassuringly at the same time.

If the horse still refuses to enter the water, don't resort to force other than a squeeze of the legs and light pressure with spurs or a tap of the whip. However, do not let the horse turn away. Keep him facing the water, signaling that forward is the only way to go. If the horse backs up, stop him with leg pressure. If he continues to back, don't resort to force to stop him. Instead, do just the opposite; ask him to back much farther down the trail than he wanted. Your job is to make the escape tactic more uncomfortable than facing the water obstacle. When you feel you've made the point that you are in charge and that continued backing is uncomfortable, ride the horse forward again. The message you are giving him is that any option other than going through the water will create discomfort. It may take some time, but this technique works with most horses.

This also is one time that you must persevere until successful. If the horse is allowed to evade the crossing, the next time you attempt it will be much more difficult. This is the reason you should plan the crossing in advance. Make certain it and the trail are safe, and make certain that you have all the time in the world to get the job done.

As mentioned earlier, you must not allow the horse to turn away from the water. To achieve this, take a firm grip on the reins — one in each hand, with hands extended out from the neck. This hold will help to keep him looking forward and prevent his turning away.

Firmness and Kindness

Remember that abuse is never the answer. The proper approach is firm, unrelenting but gentle pressure until the horse decides he at least has to try crossing the troublesome obstacle to regain a comfort zone. In the case of a small stream, the horse may rush across the first time or even attempt to leap it. That's okay, as long as he

crosses. Then, it becomes a matter of repetition — back and forth across the steam until the horse becomes desensitized, relaxes, and walks through on his own, without another horse in front.

With some horses, particularly those raised on rangeland, refusal to cross water never occurs because the horse has grown up crossing streams

Be firm and insistent in new situations.

and rough country. With others, especially those bred and raised in a stable, crossing a river for the first time can be terrifying. The rider must at this point elicit the necessary response without traumatizing the horse. Harsh whipping and spurring definitely are not the answer.

The horse relents and obeys.

One word of caution, though, when carrying out this type of training. Never, never dismount and stand in front of your horse and attempt to pull him toward you. Seeing you standing in the middle of the river might inspire the horse to think that where you are is safe. The horse is apt to cross the scary spot with a leap that will land him right in your lap. It is the same for crossing logs and other challenging spots. Never be in front of your horse.

Navigating Hills

Early in the training on the trail, you will want to expose your horse to steep hills, if at all possible. It is a general rule of thumb that horses will descend a steep slope slowly, but will try to get to the top in a hurry. There is a reason for this. It takes a horse some time to learn that its rear legs have to serve as brakes when descending a hill. In the early going let the horse pick his way down a steep slope at a pace that is comfortable for him. It's much better to travel too slowly than to go rocketing down the hill. A rapid descent can result in a fall. As the horse gains experience, he will naturally pick up the pace when descending.

When heading up a steep hill, I think it is best to keep the horse at a walk. Many horses will want to lunge up a hill so that they can use both back legs as driving forces. This can be dangerous if those back feet should encounter a rock that gives way or the trail happens to be slippery. I believe a good trail horse should be taught to walk up the hill as well as down.

This part of the training becomes especially important if you plan to be doing some mountain riding.

During your early rides on the trail, patience on your part is a real virtue. Always remember that you intend for this horse to be your trail-riding companion for years to come, so take your time. Turn your trail training into a building-blocks approach. Make sure that one block in the training regimen is firmly established and in place before adding another block in the form of a new challenge.

8

TYING AND HOBBLING
Keeping Them Where We Want Them

Whether on a pack trip into the mountains or on a weekend trail ride during which you return to your trailer at night, it is important that your trail horse has been taught to stand quietly when tied, hobbled, or tethered by one foot to a picket pin.

As you start your horse on a training routine, you might ask him to stand tied for only a short period. Tie the horse to a hitching rail or a wooden fence, groom him, and then leave him for a little while before proceeding with the training session. Do the same at the end

A trail horse must learn to stand quietly while tied.

of the session. Cool down and groom the trainee, and then let him stand tied for a bit. Do not reward the horse with grain or other treats after the end of a session of being tied. If you do, the horse will associate the end of the session with the treat and will learn impatience rather than patience with being tied.

As the training progresses, gradually lengthen the periods the horse must stand tied. You might start with five minutes and progress to an hour or more of the horse's standing unattended.

The goal is to get the horse gradually used to being confined to one spot and to accept this as a routine part of life. The important thing, especially with young horses, is to tie them in a location and in such a manner that they don't get into trouble. If the horse is tied to a post along a barbed-wire or woven-wire fence and begins pawing and extending a foreleg, for example, you are asking for a disaster that can end the horse's career before it begins.

Tying Correctly

When you are tying a horse, the key is do it securely but not so securely that you can't free him if need be. There are two basic knots for this: the simple bow knot and the bolen. Each has advantages and disadvantages. The bow knot is designed for quick release but

Tie securely, but allow for release.

can become wedged if a horse pulls back, requiring a mighty jerk from a powerful arm to free it. The bolen is really the best solution. It takes an extra moment to tie and untie, but it can't be pulled so tightly that it is impossible to free.

Make sure you tie your horse to something solid. If the horse should become frightened and pull back, you don't want a hitching rail or fence board to pull free. It doesn't take much to imagine the wreck that would ensue.

If possible, tie the horse where there is activity, such as other horses coming and going or vehicles being started and driven on and off the yard. If this practice is started when the horse is young, the animal will become desensitized to the type of activity that occurs at campgrounds and trailheads. In addition, the busy surroundings give the horse something to concentrate on.

The manner in which the horse is tied is also important. The tie rope should be long enough so that the horse doesn't feel overly confined, but not so long that he can get a front leg over the rope. A good rule of thumb is to have the tie area higher than the horse's head whenever possible.

As the horse's training program continues, and he is being tied for longer periods, try tying him near other horses. Again, this can be gradual. Begin by tying another horse nearby, but far enough away to avoid physical contact, and progress to the point where the two are tied side by side. If the companion is a horse that shared a pasture or corral, this usually is not traumatic.

However, you should always be aware of pecking order. A young horse at the bottom of the pecking order might be intimidated and frightened if the dominant horse in the band is tied beside him. When tethering your horses on a trail ride, always make certain that compatible horses are tied next to each other. This not only is good injury prevention, but also saves the timid horse from being terrorized all night long and unable to rest.

Picket Line

Eventually, trail horses should be taught to stand when tied to an overhead picket line, a rope that is stretched between two solid objects, such as trees. When horses are tied to a picket line rather than to a wooden fence or hitching rail, they have 360-degree movement. If the horse has never been so tethered at home, the first time he is picketed this way on a trail ride can be upsetting. The impor-

Tying to a picket line.

tant thing is that the picket line be high and that it be tight.

The reason for using a picket line instead of tying to trees is basic — to save the trees. Tying a horse to a tree can result in the tree's demise. First, the rope can cut into the bark. Second, the walking and pawing of the tied horse can expose and damage the tree roots.

Using a picket line cuts down on environmental damage. To further protect the tree, tie a wide band around the tree to which you can attach the picket line.

Hobbling

Once you have arrived at the point at which your trail horse stands quietly when tied to a solid object or to a picket line, it is time to

Placing hobbles on the front legs.

teach him to be hobbled. Hobbles are placed around the front legs of the horse to restrict his movement. Any of the many hobbles available will work, as long as they don't chafe the horse's legs. To prevent chafing, especially in wet conditions, we use hobbles lined with fleece or a soft fleece-like synthetic material.

Some trainers use hobbles as a form of restraint during various training procedures, such as the horse's being saddling or

Learning to accept the hobbles.

mounting the first time. I don't. I want my trail horses to accept the hobbles as a limitation to movement, not as something that forces them to stand in one spot. If they refuse to move while hobbled in a mountain meadow, they will quickly exhaust the grass supply at hand and go hungry.

Accepting Hobbles

When teaching a horse to accept hobbles, I prefer to be in a round corral that has soft dirt or sand for good footing. If a round pen isn't available, use a large grassy area devoid of rocks, trees, and brush.

By the time I introduce the horse to hobbles, he has already learned to work on a longe line and, more importantly, has developed confidence in me as the trainer and head of the pecking order.

I will lead the horse to the center of the training pen and quietly buckle on the hobbles. If the horse is a bit apprehensive, have a second person assist by holding the animal. The person putting on the hobbles is in a vulnerable position when kneeling at the horse's front end.

The hobbles are attached around the fetlocks, or just above them on the cannon bones. Once the hobbles are in place, I stand at the horse's head, reassuring it while the helper steps out of the way. Most horses will move of their own volition, and they should be given every opportunity to do so. If they refuse, have a longe whip handy and gently encourage them by flicking the whip toward their hocks. The purpose is to get the horse to move forward with the hobbles on. You want him to realize that hobbles restrict forward movement but don't prevent it.

Reactions Vary

Horses react differently to being hobbled. Some rear and lunge until they figure out they can't free themselves; others mince along quietly, unperturbed. The reason for fleece-lined hobbles becomes quickly evident if the horse struggles. The goal is to teach the horse

Learning how to move with hobbles.

to accept something that inhibits freedom of movement but does not inflict pain.

The longe line can be used to bring the horse under control if he becomes unduly frightened by the hobbles, which rarely happens. After an attempt or two to get free, most horses will accept the hobbles and learn how to move with them.

The moment I sense the horse is relaxing and gaining confidence, I unsnap the longe line and leave the training pen to let the horse learn how to cope with the hobbles on his own.

The horse may require a few sessions to become comfortable with being hobbled, but quite soon he will learn to move about with relative ease.

Some Limitations of Hobbles

The bad news about this form of restraint is that some horses learn to travel easily with them on.

Early in our mountain riding adventures, we thought it was perfectly safe to hobble our horses overnight in a meadow and leave them there until time to saddle up the next morning. After all, they could graze at their leisure all night long. Not a good idea.

During one trip in the Big Horn Mountains of Wyoming, a thunderstorm came up during the night — not an unusual occurrence when camping in the high country. We crawled from our tents the next morning and looked out at an empty meadow. Every one of our hobbled horses had disappeared. And, worst of all, the rain had washed out their tracks.

Had they gone into heavy timber or had they returned to the trailhead several long hiking hours away? We got lucky. We searched the timber first and, sure enough, there they were. We had searched an hour or more before finding them, but it sure beat walking all the way to the trailhead.

That experience, and a few more like it, taught us to put up a picket line shortly after arriving at camp. When dusk arrives now, every horse is tied to the picket line.

Picket Pin

The fact that many horses travel easily and rapidly in hobbles led me to try something that I had avoided for years — tethering the horse to a picket pin. I had always been concerned that this was a sure avenue to injury if a horse became tangled in the twenty- or thirty-foot picket rope. I am indebted to a Kentucky friend, Leonie Ommundson, a mountain outfitter turned Thoroughbred trainer, for a solution.

If you picket the horse by one back foot, she said, it won't become tangled in the picket rope. I wasn't so sure until I tried it myself. However, this is not something that should be done without a lot of preparation. Simply picketing a horse by the back foot with the other end of the picket rope attached to an immovable object is asking for injury, at least until the horse becomes accustomed to this form of restraint.

To begin the training session, I lead the horse into an open area and attach a cuff containing a ring to one rear foot. The picket line is then attached to the ring. For some reason I choose the left rear, but it

A horse tethered to a picket pin.

Holding the longe line in one hand and the picket rope in the other.

doesn't matter which rear foot is used. The cuffs that we use were cut away from a set of hobbles. They will not chafe the pasterns.

At this point you should have an assistant hold the horse with a lead rope attached to the halter. When I do it on my own, I attach a longe line to the halter and hold it in one hand and the picket rope in the other. It is important that the horse doesn't bolt and get free. If he tries to move away, I simply drop the picket line attached to the leg and pull the horse's head around with the longe line.

In the beginning I never secure the free end of the picket rope but hold it in my hand.

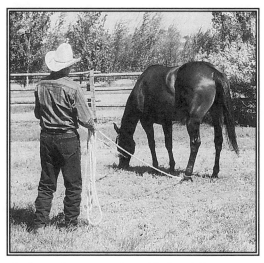

The horse learns to relax with the picket rope.

Do this early training in a grassy spot because the horse will want to graze, mimicking what will happen when he is ground picketed on a trail ride. As the horse moves about, I pick my moment and apply pressure on the rope, preventing the one rear leg from moving forward.

Expect some disagreement from the horse at this point. Usually, the horse's head will come up, and he will kick out with the confined leg in an effort to free it. When this happens, ease off on the pressure, but do not completely release it. We don't want the horse to be firmly anchored at this point, but we do want him to know that he can't do as he chooses with the confined leg, such as walk off. If the horse insists on going forward through the pressure, walk with him, but never completely release the pressure until he stops to graze again. When he lowers his head to eat, relax all pressure until he seeks to move forward once more.

Again, we are using pressure in the training process. The pressure on the picketed leg tells the horse to stop. The moment he does, the horse is rewarded with a release of pressure. Continue this pressure and release by hand until the horse stops fighting it and begins grazing in a circle around you rather than walking straight away.

This training procedure should be done over several daily sessions.

The second step, once the horse is yielding to the pressure on his back leg, is to introduce him to an object that can't be moved. Either a tree or a picket pin can be used at this point, but, in the beginning do not securely attach the end of the picket rope to the immovable object.

Instead, run the rope around the base of a tree or stake, or through the ring of the picket pin, and grip the other end. Now, when the horse reaches the end of the line, exert a bit more pressure to let him know that a limit has been reached. If the horse struggles, you can quickly free him by easing your grip on the rope.

Before long the horse will stop moving forward the moment he feels pressure. He will then back up or change course to relieve the pressure. When he is doing this with no consternation, it is time to picket hard and fast.

However, do not picket the horse and leave him to his own devices. Instead, shorten the picket rope to the point where you can tie a gentle bow knot and keep a grip on the free end. If the horse should begin to struggle, one quick pull releases the knot and the horse is free.

Double check that the area is free of stumps, other trees, and rocks. You don't want the picket rope becoming caught on another object as the horse moves about. I use an area in our front yard with a small tree as the anchor, but an open meadow and a picket pin would be better for the training sessions.

When you feel comfortable that the horse respects the pressure and is not frightened, fasten the rope to the immovable object and walk away. The first time you do this, be prepared for the horse to follow, as you have been his security blanket. If this happens, walk slowly and stop before the horse reaches the end of the picket rope. Pet him and give him reassurance that all is well. Then, step slowly forward so that if the horse follows, he feels easy pressure on the tethered leg rather than walking into it in full stride.

If the previous lessons have gone well, the horse will instantly recognize that he is unable to continue walking forward and will step back to ease the pressure. This is the point where having the horse tethered in a grassy area is an advantage. In a few moments the horse will forget about you and the picket rope's limitations and will return to grazing.

Unhurried Process

This training process should not be hurried. Take all the time in the world until the horse becomes relaxed and comfortable with being ground picketed.

If the horse is excitable and you are worried about him becoming frightened when left alone, use a light, breakable cord to attach to the immovable object in the beginning. Certainly, we don't want the horse to learn that he can get free if he bolts, but, on the other hand, that is better than his being injured.

So far, I have yet to find a horse that didn't quickly yield to being picketed by a rear foot, and I have never had one get its other three legs tangled in the rope.

There are some limitations when tethering in this manner. The main one involves space. If you tether several horses at one time, you must make certain that they can't cross each other's tether rope. If that happens, you can wind up with a dangerous entanglement.

CONDITIONING

Most people wouldn't think of getting up from a desk job and heading off into the mountains or hill country for long hikes without first getting into condition. The same should be true for your horse. Your trail horse should be conditioned to handle the type of riding you plan to do, whether that involves hour-long walks or rides of many hours through rugged terrain. If not, he could be susceptible to injury.

Basic Health Needs

Consider your horse as an athlete and companion that needs the best of care. You must tend to certain basic health care needs before getting your horse into an aggressive conditioning program. If your horse is to remain strong and sound throughout the season, he must have a balanced ration, regular hoof care, appropriate vaccinations (talk to a vet-

Your horse needs conditioning for the work.

erinarian about these because they vary by region), and regular deworming.

The problem is that some owners try to do all of the above just as the trail-riding season is about to begin. Suddenly, they remember that the hoof trimming has been neglected, that their horse hasn't been dewormed for months, and that they have lost track of the last immunization date. They also realize their horse has gotten thin during the winter months. They can feel the ribs under that coat of long hair. So, they rush to correct everything at once. They place the horse on a high-grain diet, call the farrier and instruct him to trim and shoe the horse so that it can be ridden immediately, consult the vet about vaccinations, and deworm the horse with several products simultaneously to make certain that all parasites are removed.

Such a crash program can spell disaster. If the hooves have been neglected all winter or even longer, they might not be ready for immediate shoeing. The farrier may have to trim them a bit and allow the horse to adjust to the new length before putting on shoes. I have seen horses come up lame in the wake of trimming hooves that reached an inordinate length. It isn't just the hoof that is involved. Tendons and ligaments also must adjust to the new hoof length.

Keeping the horse free of parasites should be an ongoing effort carried out in consultation with a veterinarian because geography and climate play important roles in determining which parasites you are dealing with and which dewormer is appropriate to keep them in check.

A sudden change in a horse's diet definitely invites disaster. The horse has a delicate digestive system, so any changes should be gradual and with awareness of the horse's nutritional needs. For example, most horses can exist just fine all winter on a diet of high-quality hay. However, when you begin stressing them with riding, you might need to up the energy level by adding some grain. However, if you add too much grain immediately, you are in danger of causing serious problems that can include founder and colic.

When thinking about a proper equine diet, compare the horse to an automobile. Automobiles convert the chemical energy of gasoline into mechanical energy, enabling the car to move. So it is with the horse, except that the horse is metabolically converting chemical energy from foodstuffs into energy that powers the muscles. The more energy a horse expends, the more "fuel" it needs. This fuel comes from carbohydrates and fats, which are present in greater quantity in grain than in hay.

Often, though, horses come through the off-season in good flesh and actually are too fat for strenuous exercise. Here again you must take care not to hurry the conditioning program or it might result in damage to muscles, tendons, ligaments, and even bones.

No matter what the situation, when planning your conditioning program you should be conscious of how the entire horse functions. In addition to nutrition, you should be knowledgeable about respiration, cardiovascular function, and muscle development.

During exercise the body's tissues need much more oxygen. This means that the lungs must work harder to increase the rate at which carbon dioxide is removed and oxygen is loaded into the blood. An out-of-condition horse will have a more difficult time providing this oxygen when it is stressed than will a fit horse. The problem will be exacerbated if the horse suffers a respiratory affliction such as chronic obstructive pulmonary disease (COPD). Known to many horsemen as heaves, COPD can be caused by feeding dusty hay and by housing the horse in a dust-laden environment. If you have any doubts about your trail horse's respiratory well-being, have your veterinarian examine him before beginning a conditioning program.

The cardiovascular system delivers to the tissues (via the bloodstream) oxygen from the lungs and nutrients from the digestive track. The cardiovascular system also helps regulate body temperature by carrying blood toward the skin surface where the cooling process takes place.

The heart pumps the blood through the distribution system at varying rates, depending on demand. We should no more ask the horse's heart for a sudden burst of strong activity after a long layoff than we should ask an obese, out-of-shape human to engage in strenuous activity such as shoveling snow or chopping wood. Both human and horse, when out of condition, should approach strenuous activity slowly and cautiously.

Finally, you must be aware that the muscles require gradual conditioning. Muscles comprise the largest tissue mass in a horse's body. Their functions are varied, but the function with which you are most concerned is locomotion. Muscles consist of fibers. During inactivity, these fibers become weaker. If sudden stress is placed upon them in this condition, muscular injury can result. They must be prepared for increased activity gradually with stresses being increased as the fibers strengthen.

By looking at the overall picture, you can see that as you begin to condition your trail horse, he will need more "fuel." The respiratory and cardiovascular systems must have increased function so that more oxygen and nutrients can be delivered to muscles. At the same time the number of mitochondria in the cells is increasing so that individual muscle units can use more oxygen.

A horse's skin also deserves consideration. When a horse is soft and out of condition, there is a greater chance for aggravating the skin in the form of cinch or girth soreness and even sore or irritated spots where the saddle rests. This is still another reason for approaching the conditioning process slowly and cautiously.

Take Your Time

Proper conditioning takes time. How much time will depend on the horse and its background. If the horse has been ridden a good deal in the past and has been off work for only a couple of months, you can proceed more quickly than you would with a horse that has never undergone a conditioning program. Once a horse is in good physical condition, it can withstand a few idle weeks. However, if the inactivity lasts any longer than that, the horse will begin to lose its fitness.

Let's take a look at conditioning the novice horse. You must take special precautions with this animal when beginning a conditioning program. As already mentioned, a sudden burst of activity can be harmful from a physical point of view. It can also harm the horse's mental attitude. A horse accustomed to roaming at leisure in pasture or paddock might have difficulty adjusting to an immediate and regimented work schedule. The novice horse will need some regular time off while it adjusts.

Conditioning should be gradual.

No matter how much time you can devote, the best approach is to start off at a walk with your novice or unconditioned horse. Let the horse stretch his muscles in leisurely fashion during those first rides. Those rides also should be short, and you should examine the horse for any signs of developing sores or muscle pain at the conclusion of each ride. If the horse demonstrates pain or soreness, give him some time off.

As the riding sessions continue, you can intersperse trotting with walking and even short distances of cantering or loping. After a month or two of this type of conditioning, you can pick up the pace and, if possible, introduce the horse to more challenging terrain, such as riding up hills and through sagebrush or doing some brush-popping.

Many competitive trail riders and endurance racers use the following regimen to condition their horses for competition. It isn't for everyone, because of the time involved. (Most people who ride do so for recreation and are limited in the amount of time they can spend with their horse. Obviously, if you can ride only once or twice a week, conditioning your horse will take longer than if you have unlimited time and opportunity to head out onto the trails.)

Here's the approach. Take from it what works for you and your horse.

Exercise Schedule

Week one — Start slowly, especially in spring. The first ride of the season might be just walking and slow trotting around a ring or corral. On days two and three, go for a two- or three-mile pleasure ride at a walk on an easy trail. On day four, rest. On days five, six, and seven, take longer rides, four or five miles perhaps, in easy terrain with walking and trotting interspersed. At this stage you want to be trotting for ten minutes and walking for fifteen.

Week two — Keep the workouts easy and interesting, alternating between arena riding and trail riding. By midweek you should be able to ride up to one hour at an outing, traveling at a pace — walking and trotting — that will cover between five and six miles. This means you'll be splitting your time trotting and walking. By the end of the week, you might want to seek out terrain that contains hills. Your first encounter with hills should be at the walk only.

Take an easy trail ride in the early weeks.

Week three — In the early part of this week, you should have two one-hour rides, covering five or six miles. On the third day throw in a short ride — about a half hour in length — with a lot of trotting and some loping. By this time you should be equally dividing your time walking, trotting, and loping. On the fourth day, rest. On days five, six, and seven, pick up the pace so that by the end of the week you can cover seven miles in one hour. A good approach is to trot for ten minutes and walk for five minutes. Lope for ten minutes or less and walk for five minutes.

Week four — Continue with varied workouts — some slow and easy rides over a long route, others at more speed, but covering less distance. By the end of week four, you should be able to cover ten miles in an hour and a half.

Week five — Time to pick up the pace, getting to the point early in the week where you can cover twelve miles in an hour and a half, and by the end of the week,

Work on challenging terrain by week five.

fifteen miles in two hours. In between, rest on day four and travel at a slower speed on the other days; but those rides should now be in terrain that's more hilly and rugged, helping the horse develop muscles that will be used in climbing steep hills and mountains (if you live in a mountainous area).

By the end of five weeks, your horse should be ready for any type of rugged terrain and able to travel all day at a moderate pace without tiring. On most trail rides you won't do as much trotting and loping as you did during the conditioning process, but by traveling at those varied speeds, you've thoroughly conditioned all of the horse's muscles.

Combine a sensible nutritional program with a sound conditioning plan, and within a couple of months you should have a horse that's ready for a season of trail riding. However, climate restrictions in some areas do not give riders the luxury of a couple of months to get a horse rounded into shape if they are going to enjoy the heart of

A fit horse on a competitive trail ride.

the riding season. What has been outlined is the ideal approach. It most certainly can be modified, as long as common sense is the guiding force.

10

BEFORE WE CAN TRAVEL,
We Must Load the Horse

Trail riding and trailering go hand in hand. Unless you are content to ride your trail horse around home all the time, and most of us are not, you need a horse that loads easily and travels well.

Nothing is more frustrating than to be all primed for a trip, with gear packed, pickup fueled, and enthusiasm high, only to find that your horse won't load. There is really no excuse for this if you have done some preparatory work. A horse should step calmly into a trailer with no urging other than opening the door and pointing the horse in the right direction.

Claustrophobia

Remember that horses tend to be claustrophobic by nature. They do not like to be confined in an area that doesn't permit free movement, such as a trailer. As has been mentioned already, horses are prey animals. When confined, they lose their prime weapon to escape predators — flight.

Our task as owner and caretaker is to free our horse of this concern by becoming his anchor. We must convince the horse that if he follows our direction, no harm will befall him, even when confined.

Early Training

The best time to teach a horse to load is as a foal, provided its mother sets a good example. A youngster will quickly learn from her not to fear trailers and will pop in and out with little or no hesitation.

This lesson is best taught in an open stock trailer or a trailer with the stall divider removed. The procedure is simple enough, provided that the foal has been halter broke. Simply lead the mare into the trailer and allow the foal to follow. In most cases this is all that is needed. The mare represents security, and the foal will follow her anywhere.

Assistance Needed

Sometimes this procedure requires assistance. The foal might find the interior of the trailer daunting, even though the foal's security is already inside. The youngster may get to the open door and lock up, content to be that close to its mother without venturing inside. At this point a gentle boost will usually get the job done.

Once the foal is inside, let the two of them stand quietly for a bit, then unload and repeat the procedure. After three or four sessions, the foal will have lost all fear of the trailer and will never again be a loading problem unless a bad experience changes its mind.

Loading or unloading a horse sometimes requires two people.

Unfortunately, many horses grow to adulthood without having seen the interior of a trailer. When they are asked to load for the first time, the prospect may terrify them. Other horses, for one reason or another (usually a bad experience), have become confirmed non-loaders. These are the toughest.

Different Approach

Linda and I have developed a system for loading older first-timers or problem horses. It requires time and patience, combined with gentle determination and quick, clear communication between the two of us — sometimes only a subtle sign or a single word. You should not begin a procedure such as this unless you are prepared to see it through to a satisfactory conclusion. If we attempt and fail to get a problem loader into a trailer, we have exacerbated an already serious shortcoming.

This also is one time when having several assistants with different ideas can be detrimental.

Trailer Position

Before bringing the problem loader from stable or corral, position the trailer properly and have all necessary equipment handy. Properly positioning the trailer means parking it beside a sturdy wood fence or barn wall to cut off one area of escape. If the rear of the trailer doesn't have a drop-down ramp, position it against a rise of ground or small bank so that the horse doesn't have a big step upward to enter the trailer. As in the case when teaching a foal to load, an open stock trailer or a trailer with the stall partition removed is best. The point is to do everything you can to alleviate that claustrophobic feeling that a narrow, single stall can induce.

The only pieces of equipment we use are a longe line or a long lead line and a longe whip. We begin the process slowly and easily. If the horse is a stranger to us, I spend some time scratching and petting it and simply leading it back and forth so that it sees me as friend rather than foe.

When I feel the horse relax and display signs that it is beginning to trust me, I lead it toward the trailer. At this point Linda is a quiet bystander with the longe whip. She serves as something of a barrier at the open side of the loading area.

Normal Reaction

Normally, the horse will get to the open doorway and stop. (Only a few precious times has the first-time loader simply followed me right into the trailer, making me look like a hero.) This requires time and

Encouraging a horse to load.

patience. We don't attempt to force the horse at this point. If it is standing there with braced legs, nose extended to sniff at the trailer floor, I simply stand quietly inside the trailer, talking to the horse in low, encouraging tones, with no pressure whatsoever on the longe line or lead shank. Linda stands quietly at the open side, whip lowered.

After the horse has sniffed a bit, it normally will raise its head and look about, seeking an easier answer to its dilemma, such as simply walking away from the trailer. This stage demands firmness. I do not permit the horse to leave the trailer. Nor do I attempt to pull it inside.

Instead, I merely hold the horse firmly with the longe line so that it remains in position,

Offering a reassuring pat.

facing the open trailer door. If the horse backs off a few steps, that's okay, but the moment it stops, I put gentle pressure on the lead shank to encourage it to move forward again. As soon as the horse takes a step forward, I let the longe line droop. That is its reward — release from pressure.

Tapping gently with the whip.

Positive Reinforcement

This is also the time for positive reinforcement. I will step forward, even if I have to leave the trailer, and pet and praise the horse for its positive steps. Then I back up once again and step into the trailer, resuming gentle pressure on the lead shank. The pressure is not applied steadily but is more a tug and release, tug and release. If the horse takes another step forward, I release all pressure and praise it. At this point I also begin alternating my position inside the trailer; playing out more line and backing up toward the center of the trailer so that the horse can see that nothing untoward happens when I move about inside the trailer. (This is one of the reasons for using a longe line that is twenty or thirty feet long for a lead shank. You have room for movement without running out of line).

As I work in a coaxing fashion with the horse, I must be able to read the animal's mind. Is it growing in confidence? Is it replacing its fear of the unknown with trust in me? Or, does neither of the above apply? Is it getting more determined with each passing minute not to enter the trailer? Is it getting firmer in its resolve to find an escape route?

Unfortunately, these questions have no easy answers. You must attempt to sense and feel what the horse is feeling and act accordingly.

Quick Communication

Quick and unmistakable communication between the person inside the trailer and the person on the ground is essential throughout the process. The person holding the longe line orchestrates the action because he is the one seeking to gain the horse's confidence. In addition, he is the person who can best read attitudinal changes by watching eyes, ears, and head movement.

If the horse has reached the trailer door's threshold on several occasions but has declined to set a foot inside, even though it no longer appears afraid, I will signal Linda to tap the horse gently on the rear end, just above the hocks, with the longe whip. At this point she will have the long end of the longe whip folded back in her hand so that she can tap with the firm portion of the whip.

As she taps, I will talk quietly to the horse, putting gentle tug-and-release pressure on the longe line to encourage the animal to step inside. The moment it lifts a foot to do so, the tapping stops and the pressure is released. However, if the horse steps backward, away from the trailer, the pressure is once again applied on the longe line and Linda taps it again with the whip.

Before long the horse realizes that being outside the trailer is more uncomfortable than being inside. Once the horse steps into the trailer, it is time for more petting and praise. If the horse becomes frightened at this point and wants to back out, let it. If you attempt to hold it or tie it firmly, the horse's worst fears will have been confirmed; it will feel trapped. However, the horse must not escape. Allow it to exit the trailer but seek to keep it facing the trailer — in a position for loading. Then apply pressure and load it again. Soon, it will enter the trailer and stand quietly. After a short time unload the horse and load it again, doing so until the horse goes willingly.

No Perfect System

No system is perfect, including our trailer-loading method. However, through the years Linda and I have loaded a great many horses that had never seen the inside of a trailer and many that were confirmed non-loaders. This method has always worked for us, and we have yet to injure a horse in the process. The horses trained in this manner have almost always stepped quietly into the trailer the next time they were asked.

Obviously, it is much better to train them as tykes so that entering a trailer is never an issue. But, that is not always possible.

Once an adult horse is loaded for the first time, it should be kept in the trailer long enough to relax. A short, slow trip is also good therapy at this point. The horse learns that it can stand securely even while the trailer is moving.

Driving Safely

However, if the horse has a bad experience at this point, such as the driver careening around corners or starting and stopping abruptly, all of the positive loading lessons will be lost.

I like the story told to me by a man who got involved with horses after completing a successful business career. He had long wanted to be a breeder and decided he would start on the right track by buying stock from a well-established farm.

The purchase negotiations were concluded, and the man hooked his new horse trailer behind his new pickup and went to pick up his new prized possessions.

He was a bit taken aback when the lady who owned the farm would not bring out the horses until she had taken him for a trailer ride. She insisted that he climb into the trailer and stand there while she gave him a ride down the road.

It was, he said, an experience never to be forgotten. He found himself grabbing for support as she accelerated suddenly and then applied the brakes. She took a corner at speed, and he found himself being slammed against the trailer wall.

Then she slowed the vehicle, made a gentle turn, and, gaining speed gradually, returned to the farm, where she braked to a quiet, no-jolt stop.

Please remember, she told him, what he had just experienced is how it is for many horses. They are often slammed about and physically and mentally punished by unthinking drivers. The experience, the man said, turned him into a driver who never forgot he was pulling horses, passengers that didn't know when he was going to start and stop or take a corner.

If we train a horse properly and make certain it has no traumatic experiences while traveling, it will always readily enter a trailer and travel quietly. The goal in loading a horse should be to have it enter the trailer without anyone leading it. We should be able to flip a lead rope over its neck and step aside while it loads itself. This is highly important because it might wind up in the hands of someone who has a trailer with partitioned stalls. Even with an escape door for the handler, it is dangerous to lead a horse into a single stall.

Partitioned Stalls

Once I have a horse loading easily in either a stock trailer or a trailer that has the stall partition removed, I like to teach the horse to load into a trailer where a partition separates the stall. This can be accomplished in much the same way as just discussed. I will get into the opposite stall and, if it is a two-door trailer, will close that door so the horse can't follow me. I will then seek to lead it into the adjacent stall. Usually, the horse will do this readily, but Linda will be standing by with the longe whip to provide encouragement if needed.

Once the horse is loading with no resistance, it is time for the final step. I will lead the horse to the trailer door with the longe whip in my free hand. If the horse needs encouragement, I will reach back and tap it gently just above the hocks. It won't be long before the horse will walk right up to the trailer and load itself. No longe whip will be necessary.

Unloading

While most trailering problems involve loading, unloading can also cause problems, especially from a partitioned single stall. I

This horse loads easily.

think horses should be taught to unload both ways — frontward and backward. If they are in an open stock trailer, you can allow them to turn and walk out. However, that is not an option in trailers with single stalls.

We have had experience with horses that will load easily into a single stall but panic backing out when that rear foot hits empty air. Confinement doesn't allow the horse to see what is behind it and that can foster fear and apprehension. Usually, we can cajole a horse into backing out if we take the time and trouble. The first thing to do is back the trailer against a slight bank or rise in the ground so that Mother Earth is at the same level as the rear of the trailer. This removes the need for the horse to step down into open space.

When faced with a problem unloader, snap longe lines onto each side of the horse's halter and play them out through the back door. You should have at least one assistant for this procedure, so that each of you can manage a longe line.

Again, we are going to apply pressure in an attempt to get the horse to move away from it, but we are not physically going to force the horse to leave the trailer. Working in unison, each person applies pressure on the longe line, causing the horse to move backward.

133

When the horse is about to step from the trailer, we ease the pressure somewhat and allow it to stand quietly, but not to move forward. When the horse is standing relaxed, we increase the pressure again, this time to the point where it is forced to move a rear foot to maintain balance. The goal of the handlers on the longe lines should be to prevent the horse from moving to the front of the trailer stall but still allow it to find what the horse considers solid footing inside the trailer for its rear foot.

After allowing the horse to stand quietly for a few moments, the pressure on longe lines is once again increased. This time the goal is to get the horse to step back to the point where the foot touches firm ground that is about the same level as the trailer. Obviously, if that rear foot hits ice or slippery mud instead of firm ground, the problem is greatly compounded.

With time, patience, and firm, but kind pressure, you should soon have the horse backing from the trailer. Once that is accomplished, it is time for some repetition. The horse should be loaded and unloaded until it no longer fears backing out. Then, the trailer should be moved and the horse unloaded in a spot where the distance between the trailer floor and ground is greater. The two longe lines might have to be employed the first time the horse is asked to step down, but it will now learn quickly, and there should be little or no resistance after the first effort.

CROSS-COUNTRY HAULING
Getting from Here to There

The obvious reason you teach a horse to load and unload is so that you can haul it from Point A to Point B. This could mean from home to a neat trail five miles down the road, or it could mean a trip that involves a thousand miles or more.

The short trips are easy, providing you have a horse that loads and unloads easily. You simply put it into the trailer, drive to your destination, unload, tack up, and go for a ride.

It isn't quite that easy when you travel many hundreds of miles. When that is the case, there are details that must be attended to.

Pulling Power

A basic consideration is pulling power. You might get by just fine with a light car or pickup towing a loaded two-horse trailer for a short trip on level ground, but what about a trek that requires you to cross a mountain range? You might discover, after it is too late, that you didn't have the necessary power to get that trailer up long, steep inclines.

On our first trip into the mountains, I found myself woefully short of pulling power, and it was a daunting experience. We were traveling into the Big Horn Mountains near Buffalo, Wyoming. The pull from Buffalo to the trailhead is about fifteen miles, all of it on a steep incline. We were still a mile or so from the trailhead when my pickup simply came to a stop, unable to pull the four-horse trailer any higher.

Make sure you have enough pulling power for the trip.

Fortunately, we were already off the highway and on the final approach, a dirt road. We unloaded the horses, and members of the group rode them bareback the rest of the way to our jumping-off point. Without the horses I was able to make it the rest of the way. Don't find out you have insufficient pulling power after the fact.

Perhaps the key element when traveling with horses, however, is the trailer itself. This is true whether you are driving one mile or one thousand. You must have a trailer that is safe, not only for the horse it is carrying, but for other motorists on the highway as well.

Horses in trailers defecate and urinate just as they do in stalls at home. However, in a trailer some of that urine and the moisture from manure become trapped between the mat and wooden flooring. Over time the wet conditions cause the wood to rot, and rotted floorboards pose a serious danger to the horse. Horror stories abound concerning horses that have stepped through a rotten plank on the floor of a trailer, severely damaging hooves and legs. From the horse's point of view, nothing is more important than solid flooring.

Preventive Maintenance

You should carry out preventive maintenance, such as cleaning out the trailer after each trip and rolling back the mats so that the wooden flooring can dry properly, but time will still take its toll. Frequently checking the flooring and replacing any boards that are suspect are musts.

Use a large screwdriver or some other sharp object to poke and prod the flooring, particularly at the sides where moisture is most easily trapped. If you feel a soft spot anywhere, replace that board.

Check the Lights and Brakes

You also should check the trailer's lights and brakes. Some unseen force seems to be at work to keep trailer lights and brakes from working properly. Actually, that force is nature, battering fragile wires with mud, water, debris, and bumpy roads until something gives way or shorts out. Heading down a long, steep hill with a four-horse trailer without brakes can produce a dangerous situation for everyone in the vicinity. It is the same with lights. If signal lights or brake lights don't work, you are setting the stage for a serious accident.

Before leaving home, have someone stand behind the trailer while you check running lights, brake lights, and signal lights. Check the brakes by rolling slowly ahead and then manually applying the trailer brakes. It is only in this way that you can tell for sure if they are working. (Most trailer brakes include a unit located just under the dash. You can manually apply the brakes using this unit.)

Next, try the brakes on both the trailer and the truck by applying the brakes of the pulling vehicle. They should function in synchronization. You don't want the trailer brakes locking up with tires squealing while the towing vehicle is still rolling along. Instead, the trailer brakes should exert pressure equivalent to that of the towing vehicle's brakes.

When the braking force is equal on trailer and towing vehicle, the whole combined unit remains in a line.

Using Brakes

Simply having brakes is not enough. You must learn how to use them correctly. For example, when driving on ice, you should never jam on the brakes but should use a pumping motion to prevent skids.

Driving at speeds that are appropriate for the road conditions can negate the need for heavy braking. Even then you must never forget that a load of horses in a trailer is a heavy pushing force that sometimes even the best braking system can't stop.

I was pulling a loaded six-horse trailer over nearly 10,000-foot Togwotee Pass in the Bridger-Teton Mountains of Wyoming. As we climbed toward the pass, traveling west to east, it began to snow. The higher we got, the heavier the snow and the more slippery the highway. I shifted into four-wheel drive for both safety and added traction.

The going was slow and torturous, but finally we crested and began the equally steep descent. This was no time to relax because gaining too much speed would be more dangerous than anything we had faced in climbing up the other side. I shifted to low gear.

All was going well until we rounded a curve and there, stuck in the highway in front of us, was a semi-truck loaded with round hay bales. The truck had spun out in the attempt to reach the summit.

I began pumping the brakes and though I was only going about fifteen miles per hour, the weight of the trailer and the load of horses, combined with what was by then glare ice on the highway, made stopping impossible. I couldn't see if there was a vehicle coming around the stalled semi. If I went around him, I was risking a head-on collision. There was a drop-off on the right side of the road and a cliff wall on the left.

I made a decision. I would crash the front of the truck into the cliff wall rather than risk a head-on collision. As I started steering toward the cliff wall, the semi driver raced from the rear of the truck to the front and waved for me to go by. He had heard me coming slowly down the mountain before I rounded the curve and had run to the rear of the truck to stop traffic. We slipped between the semi and the drop-off to the right and heaved a big sigh of relief.

Trailer Hitch

The ball, whether a bumper hitch or fifth wheel, is also a key to safety. If the ball on the pickup bed or hitch is too small, you can wind up with an unattached trailer careening wildly out of control, posing a threat to the horses inside and to anyone else on the road.

Make sure the hitch fits the ball.

One way to find out if the ball properly fits the trailer hitch is to fasten it in place and then apply pressure with the support shaft and wheel used to raise and lower the front of the trailer. If you put strong upward pressure on the ball and it raises the rear end of the car or pickup instead of coming free, you should be in good shape.

Check Tires

Tires, too, can be a source for discomfort and disaster. For some reason many trailer owners seem to think they can put any kind of "rubber" on a trailer and head off down the road, blissfully believing that all will be well.

The result can be a flat that is, at the least, inconvenient and frustrating, and, in some cases, downright dangerous. For a couple of summers, we seemed to be having an inordinate number of flats — three during one cross-country trip alone.

After several years of this annoyance, I was so fed up that I bit the financial bullet and bought four steel-belted radials for the trailer. The tire merchant thought I was crazy. You don't need those expensive tires, he argued. Yes, I do, I argued back. I am sick and tired of flats on the road. For the next three years, we had nary a flat.

I'm not saying that you should run out and buy steel-belted radials for your trailer, but if you do a lot of long-distance hauling they can be a good investment. At the least you should make certain that the trailer tires are in as good condition as the tires on the car or pickup pulling it.

Repacking the wheel bearings on the horse trailer is also an important matter and should be done annually. The best time is in the spring before a new season of travel begins. A burned-out wheel bearing can, in the worst-case scenario, result in a wheel coming off, totally wrecking the trip and perhaps the trailer with its load of horses. The expense involved in having a local repair shop or garage repack the wheel bearings is well worthwhile.

Care of Horses on the Road

When it comes to horse care when traveling cross-country, there are about as many opinions as there are travelers. Some owners tube their horses with oil before heading out on a long trip to make certain the animals don't become impacted. Others insist on stopping every certain many miles to unload and exercise the horses. Still others feel that stopping and unloading are a waste of time and never unload until reaching a destination, no matter what the distance.

If you are going to stop and unload, a good rule of thumb is to do it at eight-hour intervals at the least. The important thing is that you pick a safe place for the unloading and reloading. If it is winter and the stopping area is covered with ice, unloading may produce more harm than good.

You should also be aware of the surroundings. Unloading in an area where heavy trucks are whizzing by or where there is a good deal of vehicular traffic of any kind produces potential for problems. Make certain the ground is dry and that you are in a quiet area

Use extreme caution when unloading while en route to your destination.

before you ask the horses to step out of the trailer. A good plan is to check with someone at the service station where you are fueling. Inquire about the possibility of a fairgrounds or rodeo grounds in the vicinity. If the attendant doesn't know, ask for a telephone directory and call the chamber of commerce. If there is no chamber office, call a feed or tack store; the employees will know.

Once you have the horses out of the trailer, walk them about for a time so that they can stretch their muscles and relax.

Removing Urine

If possible after unloading, you also should clean the urine spots from the trailer. Urine contains ammonia that can be detrimental to a horse's respiratory system. Perhaps the worst bedding to put in a trailer when traveling is straw because it produces a multitude of dust particles and compounds rather than alleviates the ammonia problem. The most absorbent of all trailer bedding materials is peat moss. Lacking that, you can turn to wood shavings, which are next in efficiency and safety.

Chapter 11

Individual Approach

You must always remember that horses are individuals. Yes, we sometimes travel for long periods without unloading, but only with veteran horses that have been over thousands of miles of highways and are relaxed in the trailer.

If, however, we introduce a young horse into that equation, it could change our approach. A young, inexperienced traveler might remain tense and nervous the entire trip. With this type of horse, we stop frequently, unload, and reload just to get the horse to relax.

Feeding When Traveling

Horse owners vary on feeding when traveling. Some withhold feed before and while traveling. Others feed the ration the horse is used to when at home. The best approach, in my opinion, is to pretty much keep the horse on its normal diet. However, because we often travel cross-country in a stock trailer, we feed only hay while on the road. No grain until we stop for the night.

You must never forget that it is the horse's nature to consume food in small quantities but to do so frequently. Horses that are used to eating frequently will become stressed if deprived of food for long hours and could even colic.

Leg Wrap Dangers

Some owners insist on wrapping their horses' legs in bandages as extra support. I do not favor leg wraps. They compromise the normal functioning of the tendons and can curtail normal blood flow. When they are released from the bandages, the tendons are in a weakened state, and if the horse undergoes vigorous exercise, tendon injury can result. Compromising the blood flow puts the horse's foot in jeopardy as the foot requires a flow of blood to remain healthy.

We also never "oil" our horses. I don't really think it is necessary for a healthy horse, and a number of veterinarian acquaintances agree with that position. Besides, getting a tube through the nose and into the stomach to dump a quart or more of liquid is pretty stressful for a horse.

Watering on the Road

Often one of the most frustrating aspects of traveling cross-country with horses involves watering them.

In our experience no matter what we do with water or to water, some horses drink very little on the road. If the day is hot, we keep a bucket handy, and when we stop to fuel up, we offer them water in the trailer. More often than not, they will sip instead of drink heartily unless temperatures are soaring.

We had one female pack mule that simply refused to drink when we traveled. We could unload after a full day of travel and set a bucket of fresh water in front of her. She wouldn't even sniff it. She just went to munching on hay. We worried about impaction and kidney problems the first time we traveled cross-country with her and tried every trick we could think of to get her to drink. She turned up her nose at our every ploy and went back to eating hay.

Finally, we decided it was an idiosyncrasy we would have to live with. Usually, on the first day of a ride into the mountains, she would stop at a stream and tank up, none the worse for wear. However, I consider her to have been an unusual animal, and every possible effort should be made to get horses and mules to consume water when traveling.

The problem when animals refuse to drink is that they are in danger of suffering damage to the kidneys. This is especially true of older horses. They should be watered at least every two hours while traveling. Without proper intake of water, the horse loses potassium and other electrolytes. An undue loss of potassium can bring on muscle tremors and weakness.

One approach is to place something in the water at home that overrides the normal taste. Thus, when you stop to water them, the horses are tasting a substance flavoring the water to which they have become accustomed. Frequently a can of carbonated soda, such as Coke or Pepsi, will do the trick. Gatorade can also be effective. The important thing is we make certain the horses are used to drinking the "doctored" water before we ever leave home.

Heat Buildup

While stopping to offer water to horses and allowing them to relax and urinate are important, there is also a downside.

A metal or fiberglass trailer standing still in the sunshine builds up heat rapidly. Added to this particular discomfort factor is body heat from four or more horses. Before long, discomfort turns into the danger of heat exhaustion.

Stopping ten minutes or more can send internal temperatures soaring to 110 degrees and higher if the trailer is parked in the hot sun. Air flow through a moving trailer helps dissipate the heat. Thus, common sense must be employed. Yes, we want to stop for perhaps half an hour to allow the horses to rest and relax. But, no, we won't always stop that long if a hot sun is beating down on the trailer.

Proper Ventilation

Proper trailer ventilation is critical when traveling; the more the better. If there is too little ventilation in the summer, heat can build to an intense level even when the trailer is on the move. If there is too little ventilation during winter travel, a condensation of moisture and steam can form and distress a horse's respiratory system.

This stock trailer has plenty of ventilation.

Early training of the trail horse in a round pen.

As part of its training, the horse must learn to stand quietly while tied.

The trail horse must accept the rider's mounting from both sides.

Riding alone on the trails helps build the
horse's confidence.

A good trail horse willingly crosses water.

Downed timber and water can be common obstacles.

Kathy and Rick Swan

Crossing a bridge requires single formation.

Kathy and Rick Swan

Even when there is room on the trail, someone should always lead.

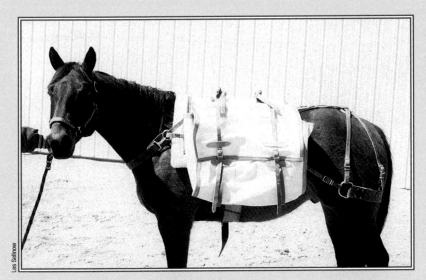

A packhorse outfitted with the proper equipment.

Ideally, a rider should not lead more than one packhorse.

Make sure truck and trailer can handle mountainous terrain.

Setting up camp at the trailhead.

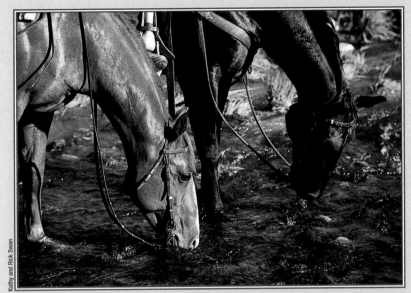

Allow the horses to drink freely when on the trail.

Only permit your horse to graze after you have dismounted.

Be alert when riding and camping in bear country.

Make sure the campsite is fairly level and protected.

Tying horses to a picket line cuts down on environmental damage.

Knowing where you packed provisions saves time.

Marilyn Hahn

Fishing for dinner provides a bountiful yield.

Kathy and Rick Swan

Cooking over the campfire.

Caring for saddles under a protective tarp.

A tarp also can provide shelter from the elements.

After water is purified, it is suspended in a plastic container.

Take time to enjoy the beauty of your surroundings.

Setting out for the next day's ride...

...and soon falling into a workable formation.

Traveling across taxing terrain can cause your saddle to slip.

Readjust the saddle to avoid making your horse sore.

Linda Sellnow

A trail horse in training follows a veteran across his first bridge.

Sharon Warwick

Traverse rivers and streams with care.

Weather can change quickly in the mountains.

A campfire at day's end can take off the chill.

Having enough ventilation is easily accomplished when pulling a stock trailer where the top one-eighth or more of the side walls are open. It is sometimes more difficult when pulling an enclosed trailer. Many of these have roof ventilators and side windows that slide open. My rule of thumb when using these trailers during daytime summer travel is to open all windows and vents to allow as much air as possible to circulate.

Urination Problem

While we have been fortunate in avoiding serious problems when traveling, they can occur. I remember one trail ride where a friend arrived with a prize show stallion. He decided it was time for the horse to learn about the great outdoors. The horse was tied to the trailer for the night. It was soon obvious that the stud was in serious distress.

The owner quickly diagnosed the problem. The horse had not urinated since leaving home. We decided that the problem was the strange environment. At that time I was living about fifteen miles from that particular trail-riding site and had a stable with box stalls, a more familiar environment to the horse. We loaded him up, hauled him to the stable, and put him in a box stall bedded with straw. A few minutes later, the horse stretched out and urinated. With his discomfort gone, he began to munch hay.

The first line of attack when you have a horse that won't or can't urinate would be to get the horse into a quiet and comfortable situation, such as a well-bedded box stall. However, this sometimes isn't possible if you have arrived at a trailhead, miles from town.

If you suspect that the problem might occur, it might be wise to include furosemide (Lasix is a brand name and is now called Salix), a diuretic often used on racehorses, in the medicine kit. It can be administered intramuscularly and is quite effective in getting a horse to urinate within a short period after being administered. However, you should consult with a veterinarian in advance concerning the efficacy of this approach.

Know Your Horse

A key to understanding and/or detecting problems with your horses when on the road is observation. Each horse is an individual and will react to stress or problems in its own unique manner. You must know your horses so that when they give you a signal that all is not well, you will instantly understand the communication.

If, for example, your horse is one that is always alert and conscious of anything new in its environment, you should become immediately concerned if it steps from the trailer and doesn't bother to look around or stands with droopy ears.

It is the same with the animal's gait. When you unload, lead the horse around for a bit and observe it. The horse may take a moment to regain its land legs, but watch carefully for any sign of lameness.

This is also a good time to run your hands over the horse's body, especially its legs. Are there any signs of heat that might indicate inflammation? Does the horse flinch when you put even gentle pressure on its tendons? Check the nose and eyes. Is there nasal discharge? Are the eyes dull and weepy instead of bright and shiny? Horses will tell you how they feel; you just have to be able to understand what they are saying.

If possible, have the phone number of a veterinarian at the selected stopover spot. Something amiss may mean the animal's good health is in danger, and you can call for professional help. You may wind up spending an extra day for the horse to recuperate, but that is far better than winding up at your destination with a sick or lame horse.

PROPER EQUIPMENT

Well-meaning trail riders often punish their horses with improper or ill-fitting equipment, ranging from bridles and bits to saddles. A bit in the horse's mouth and a saddle on its back are already foreign objects. However, they are necessary "evils" for the horse if we are to enjoy trail riding in safety and comfort.

There is little or no excuse for an improper bit or ill-fitting bridle, but saddles are a more complicated matter. The traditional saddle is basically a fixed object with little flexibility. The horse's back, on the other hand, bends, moves, and flexes as the animal stops, starts, and changes direction. So we need to take extra care in ensuring that a saddle fits the horse.

The saddle-fit problem is compounded because one size doesn't fit all. The saddle that might be just right for a broad-withered Quarter Horse or Arabian might be totally wrong for a high-withered Thoroughbred or American Saddlebred.

Complicating matters further is that as the trail-riding season progresses, your horse's body changes shape. Usually after a winter of relative idleness, you start with a somewhat overweight, flabby-muscled horse. The horse needs to be conditioned and muscled up gradually before you head out on a long trail ride.

So, you saddle up and begin the process. However, your saddle isn't going to rest on the horse's back the same way it will when the flab disappears and the muscles firm up and strengthen.

As the season wears on, the horse's body will take on a third shape, becoming even leaner and more streamlined if you ride a great deal. Therefore, during one riding season you are placing your saddle aboard three different anatomical configurations even though only one horse is involved. The result can be a sore-backed horse somewhere along the way.

So, what is the answer? Do you need a different saddle for each stage of equine body development?

Fit Condition

The answer is to use a saddle that fits properly when the horse is fit and to avoid making the horse sore until it reaches that point of fitness. This is accomplished by systematic and gradual conditioning.

Interestingly, many ancient warriors, such as the warriors of Attila the Hun, did not use saddles during their travels and battles, even though saddles were very much around in that era. Instead these warriors rode bareback, wrapping their torsos to prevent sore back muscles and their legs to prevent chaffing.

The reason was basic. They feared that saddles hurt their horses' backs during long-distance treks. Without a sound horse to ride, the warriors would be helpless.

Cowboys of the American West used saddles far different from today's pleasure saddles. Those early saddles had a short seat, with a high pommel and cantle. (The pommel includes the swells and horn at the front of the saddle, and the cantle is the raised area in the rear.) I learned to ride in such a saddle. It was a seat that provided rider security and probably was more comfortable for the horse than many modern saddles. The comfort to the horse stemmed from the fact that the saddle was short and fit that portion of the back suited to carrying a saddle without impinging shoulder movement.

Saddles Changed

Saddles changed with the coming of the automobile. No longer were cowboys required to spend long days on a horse. The new influences on saddle makers were rodeo contestants and pleasure riders. Calf ropers, for example, looked for a saddle from which they could dismount quickly. The high cantle had to go. Pleasure riders were more concerned with their riding comfort than with security. The high pommel and high cantle did not figure into this scenario.

Pommels and cantles were lowered and seats lengthened to provide more room for the derriere. These changes brought problems for the horse.

Some saddles are simply too long for a horse's back. Riders tend to push the too-long saddle forward, cinch it down, and climb aboard. After riding in such a saddle for a fairly long period, they wonder why the horse is walking with a shortened stride in front and why it displays displeasure and discomfort every time it is saddled.

Proper Placement

Putting the saddle too far forward is a basic reason for a sore riding horse. To understand why, stand back and watch an unsaddled horse move. Concentrate on the shoulders. You will notice that the scapula or shoulder bone is a moving element. As the front leg moves forward, the scapula moves rearward within its setting of muscles, ligaments, tendons, and nerves. In some horses this movement is up to four inches toward the rear.

The saddle should leave the shoulders free.

Placing a saddle too far forward on a horse and cinching it down set the stage for discomfort and even pain. The saddle and rider's weight put pressure on the scapula with its every movement. Another problem immediately surfaces with the saddle set too far

This saddle is properly positioned.

forward — the pommel becomes unnaturally high, especially in an English saddle. This makes for rider imbalance. The rider is on a saddle with the seat sloping down toward the cantle, his legs too far forward, and his seat out of balance with the horse's movements.

Because of the rearward slope design of many western saddles, however, the saddle might appear to be in proper position even though it is too far forward.

To obtain a correct fit, the saddle should be moved back to the point where the scapula has freedom of movement. Moving the saddle back off the shoulder blades also increases the contact area of that portion of the saddle that rests against the horse's back and bears weight. It is important that the weight is distributed and not settled over only a few pressure points.

With some long western saddles on short-backed horses, another problem can surface when you move the saddle back — the skirt (the leather sides of the saddle) digs into the loin area, also causing discomfort and pain.

If you move your saddle into the proper position on the horse's back and it looks totally out of balance, such as the saddle tipped forward or the skirts too far back, you just might have to face the fact you need a different saddle.

Wide Pommel

The second most common problem in saddle fitting is a pommel so wide that it rests against the horse's withers.

That bony portion of the spine is in no way designed to carry weight or sustain pressure. Only a thin layer of skin and nerves lies between saddle contact and bone. A saddle resting against the top of the withers means instant discomfort for the horse and debilitating soreness over the long haul. The saddle should sit squarely, supported by bars or panels, with no contact on the spine.

Many riders attempt to solve a wide pommel problem by adding more or thicker pads. All they usually accomplish is creating new pressure points that lead to soreness. However, a cutout pad, if riders have to make a choice, is better than having the pommel resting on top of the withers. The cutout area would

The pommel should clear the withers.

be directly beneath the pommel. This means that the sides of the saddle would be supported by the pad and there would be clearance between the pommel and the withers.

Narrow Pommel

A problem totally opposite that of the overly wide pommel is a saddle with the pommel too narrow for the horse. An example might be transferring a saddle that fits properly on a high-withered Thoroughbred to a thick-withered Arabian or Quarter Horse.

Now we have a saddle sitting too high on the horse's back and creating pressure points that will quickly become tender and sore. A too-narrow pommel used with a thick pad makes a bad situation worse. It is like putting on a thick pair of socks and then pulling on shoes that are already too small.

Check For Fit

How do you know if you are riding your trail horse with an ill-fitted saddle? First, place the saddle on your horse without blanket or pad. Move it into position so that it is not resting on the shoulder blades. Is it sitting squarely on the horse's back? Does it look balanced from front to rear?

If everything looks right, you are on the correct track. Next, however, comes the critical checklist after each trail ride. Look for the following:

- Obvious sores at any point along the back where the saddle comes into contact;

- White hairs on either side of the withers or along either side of the spine;
- Swelling or bumps along the back;
- Scars or hard spots in the muscle or skin;
- Atrophy or shrinking of muscles on the sides of the withers.

A narrow pommel can cause discomfort.

If there are sores on the horse's back, you know for certain that one of two things, or maybe both, are to blame — a saddle that doesn't fit correctly or a rider that is sitting the saddle incorrectly, such as riding lopsided with most of the rider's weight distributed to one side or the other.

The white hairs are also unmistakable signs of a problem. They appear as the result of undue pressure from the saddle at certain points along the back. The pressure alters the hair follicle, producing a white hair. If the damage is minor and the pressure removed, the white hairs may disappear with the next coat change. However, if the damage to the hair follicle is severe, the white spots will be there forever. We see this many times on roping horses but all too often on trail horses as well.

Temporary swellings usually show up immediately after removal of the ill-fitting saddle. The swelling results from damage to tender tissues because of poor saddle fit or a rider who is sitting unbalanced.

Back Palpation

If a visual examination reveals nothing obvious, it doesn't necessarily mean the horse is devoid of back pain. The only way you will know for sure is to palpate the back muscles three to four inches on either side of the spine. Just run your fingers over this area, gently applying pressure. You must, of course, be able to differentiate between normal and abnormal reactions to palpation. Most horses will flex their backs when you exert pressure, but there is a differ-

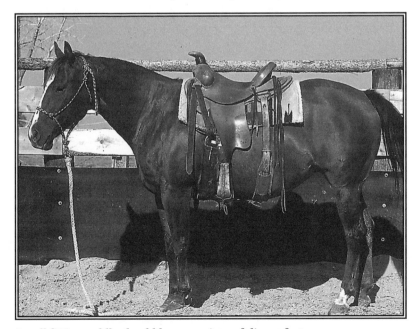

A well-fitting saddle should leave no signs of discomfort.

ence. The pain-free horse will not exhibit serious flinching or a dramatic sinking away from touch as often happens when you palpate a sore-backed horse.

Study Conformation

Study your horse's conformation and get in tune with his reactions. If he doesn't like being saddled, don't accept this as just one of his idiosyncrasies. Attempt to determine the reason. If he throws his head into the air when you mount, even on a loose rein, the horse might be telling you that his back hurts. If he walks with a short, stiff stride, he might be saying that the saddle is resting atop his shoulder blades, producing painful pressures.

When buying a saddle, don't commit unless you are sure that it will fit, even if you have to haul your horse to the saddle shop and try the saddle on him. Some merchants will allow you to take a saddle home and try it on your horse as long as you put a clean blanket beneath the saddle and use your own cinch.

I have used a variety of saddles for trail riding, including an old McClellan army saddle, a broad-purpose English saddle, a cutting saddle, and a typical western saddle. Personally, I favor a western saddle with a high rear cantle and narrow swells, the rounded portion of the pommel, in front — a slick-fork or A-frame. The high rear cantle helps me keep proper position when climbing steep slopes, and the narrow swells allow for more freedom of movement and comfort.

Linda and I each have several saddles, designed for different types of horses. During ten years of living in Kentucky, we became involved in eventing competitions — dressage, cross-country jumping, and stadium jumping. We needed an English saddle for this type of competition. During this time, we also were riding Thoroughbreds, so our western saddles were designed to fit their conformation. This meant a relatively narrow gullet. In addition, I was involved in cutting so I needed a cutting saddle with its relatively flat seat and long, narrow saddlehorn.

Our move to Wyoming ended our involvement in eventing. I continued to cut for a time, and we both continue to trail ride. However, some of our new horses had broader withers than the Kentucky Thoroughbreds. This meant adding yet another saddle to accommodate them.

If we are riding a horse with high, narrow withers, we use one saddle. If we are riding a horse with broad withers, we use a different saddle.

One of the reasons we favor the western saddle for trail riding is that we can easily attach saddlebags and tie on a slicker in case of rain.

Other Equipment

Next, let's turn to such things as breastplates, rear cinches, cruppers, and breechings. Are they necessary? A breastplate, which attaches to each side of the saddle and goes around the chest, is designed to prevent a saddle from slipping to the rear. A breastplate can be a real help in the mountains, but you must make certain that the saddle is in the proper position first. If a tightly fastened breastplate prevents a saddle from sliding rearward off the shoulder blades, for instance, you are compounding an already serious problem. The breastplate should only come into play when you are negotiating a notoriously steep incline.

Conversely, a crupper beneath the tail or breeching around the rear quarters and attached to the saddle should prevent a saddle from slipping forward and over the horse's neck. Again, the only time this equipment should come into play is when you are going down a steep incline. Neither should inhibit the horse's freedom of movement in any way.

On some horses these pieces of equipment are unnecessary, but on others, with little or no withers and a round-bodied conformation, they may be necessities. This is especially true of mules that often have low, rounded withers.

A tight rear cinch is important for roping but is not a necessity for trail riding. It is one of those things that are merely a matter of preference.

Bridles and Bits

There are thousands of bits on the market, each one proclaimed as the very best for this or that specific use. My approach to bits is this — use whatever produces the lightest pressure possible and still elicits the desired response.

Back when I used to retrain problem horses, I would frequently be sent horses whose owners couldn't prevent them from running off, even though the riders were using a very severe bit. Did I, they would inevitably ask, know of a tougher bit that could stop the horse? My approach to the problem was always the same. I would toss aside the severe bit and fit the horse with a snaffle.

A bit should fit the mouth.

If a horse decides to run off, the severity of the bit is not going to be a solution. You must first determine why the horse is running off and direct its actions and forward motion in such a manner that it no longer needs to leave the vicinity at speed. I have found that I can do this far better with a simple snaffle than with some long-shanked, high-port curb.

Whatever your choice, a trail-riding bit should fit the horse's mouth. If, for example, you have a horse with a wide face and muzzle, you will be doing him a serious injustice by putting a four and a half-inch Arabian bit in his mouth. This horse might need a bit that is five inches wide. Conversely, the five-inch bit might be too wide and uncomfortable for a narrow-muzzled horse.

Chin Strap or Chain

You can inflict a good deal of pain on your trail horses by having an improperly fitted chin strap or chain. The major mistake is having it too tight. A long-shanked curb bit and a very tight chin strap put severe pressure on the horse's tongue and bars (that area of the mouth where there are no teeth) each time you pull back.

Conversely, a too-loose strap or chain gives little or no leverage. A good rule of thumb is to make certain you can easily insert two fingers between the inside of the strap or chain and the exterior of the horse's jawbone.

I had a problem horse brought to me once because the owner said that every time she tried to bring the horse to a stop, it reared on its hind legs. I asked to see her bridle. It contained a long-shanked hackamore that featured hard rawhide around the nose and a chain beneath the animal's jaw that was pulled tight. Each time she took up on the reins, she inflicted great pain on the horse's nose and jaw, and it was rearing to avoid it. After a few weeks of being ridden in a snaffle bit, the horse forgot about rearing. To the best of my knowledge, she never rode the horse with a hackamore again.

This isn't to say that every trail horse should spend its working life with only a snaffle. Some horses need an added bit of pressure that a curb bit provides. While the snaffle applies pressure only to the tongue and corners of the mouth, the curb also applies pressure to the sensitive bars.

Bridle Adjustment

Bridle adjustment is also a key element to a proper equipment fit. The bit should rest against the corners of the lips but not be so tight that the corners wrinkle. Wrinkling means constant pressure on the lip corners, which will result in a mouth-sore, irritable horse.

On the other hand, a bit hanging an inch or more below the lip corners is going to bang on the horse's teeth. This, too, will cause discomfort and pain.

The bit and bridle you use in the horse's mouth or on its head must be comfortable. A broke four-year-old trail horse I bought provides a case in point. It was obvious at the outset that the gelding hadn't had much training. I started him in a snaffle as I do all young horses, but he wasn't keen on it. I switched to the shanked double-broken snaffle that worked so well on my cutting mare. He didn't like it. Next I tried a straight-bar grazing bit with a light chin strap. That was better, but he still wasn't happy with the bit. I tried a mild curb. He didn't like that either. I wasn't trying to accomplish something specific with the various bits. I was simply trying to find something that he would accept.

On a whim I slipped on a light bosal (a bitless bridle). I swear he almost grinned, he was so happy. There was just something about having a bit in his mouth that he couldn't tolerate, no matter what type it was.

A trail ride might last for hours, and if the horse is wearing an uncomfortable bit it soon will become irritable, tossing its head and traveling unevenly. A comfortable bit and a properly fitting saddle can make all the difference in the rider's and horse's enjoyment.

13

TRAVEL SUPPLIES

When we are leaving on a weekend trail ride, our goal is to have everything go well — no problems, just enjoyment. Making certain we have the right kind of supplies can go a long way, even when returning to a campground each night.

Forgetting something as basic as a flashlight when you have a flat tire on the highway at night, for example, can be disastrous, or as happened to us on one trip, having a flat tire and discovering that neither the tire wrench nor the jack we carried in the pickup was appropriate for a newly purchased trailer. We remain indebted to a couple of Good Samaritan cowboys who stopped and lent a hand.

During our horse showing years, my daughter, Pam, who also showed horses, took care of these details. Well before each show, she would prepare a

Tack is one essential for a trip.

159

meticulous list of everything we needed. As each item was packed or loaded before leaving home, she would check it off the list.

Itemized List

When making an itemized list, start with the most basic articles. If you are going to ride, you need a saddle, pad, and bridle. Those are really basic. But how about a hoof pick, water bucket, feed pan, brushes? The best solution to avoid forgetting any of these basics is to have them all — except for buckets and feed pans — in a carrying caddy. Thus, one item contains all the grooming supplies. However, if we have taken items from the caddy between rides and haven't returned them, we are still going to be in trouble. Check each item in the caddy before putting the carrying case on the trailer.

Will the nights be cold where you are camping? Better put in the horse blankets. How about an extra halter for each horse and extra lead ropes? Accidents can happen and equipment can break. How about insect repellent? If it is the middle of fly and mosquito season, insect repellent is a must.

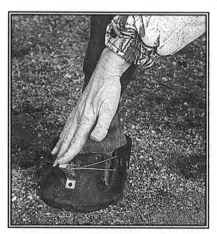

Be prepared to deal with a thrown shoe.

Throwing a Shoe

What if your horse throws a shoe and there is no farrier at the site? Do you have extra shoes and equipment to nail one on? If you don't do your own farrier work, consider carrying a commercial snap-on shoe, such as an EasyBoot. It can get you all the way through the weekend or even longer if need be.

Even with the EasyBoot, at least one person in the group should know something about basic farrier work and have a few tools along. If, for example, the horse pulls a shoe but nails are protruding from the hoof, you should have something along to pull them out.

All-Purpose Tool

I have found those all-purpose tools that fold together and are carried in a small pouch that can be attached to a belt to be indispensable. The tool will normally include a little corkscrew, a screwdriver, a knife blade, miniature scissors, and, most importantly, pliers, which can cut wires.

I remember one outing sometime back that convinced me of the importance of carrying such a tool. I was riding a rather high-strung mare on a group trail ride. Someone suggested that we take a shortcut across a field covered with high grass.

The mare I was riding became fidgety in the group, so I moved off to the side. Suddenly, it was as though we were engulfed in the tentacles of a monster. Lying hidden beneath the tall grass was a ball of wire. The mare tried to spin away from it, but that only served to entrap all four legs. I spoke to her quietly and reassuringly while wondering how in the world I was going to get out of the predicament.

She stood there quivering in fear but didn't move. I could see that I would have trouble dismounting because wire was on both sides.

One of my companions called out to sit tight and not dismount. He got off his horse and made his way to us on foot. He was a good horseman and moved quietly and talked gently to the mare as he approached. He was carrying a tool on his belt that contained a wire cutter. Carefully he snipped away at the wire, freeing the mare's legs one at a time. Planning ahead averted a potential disaster for my nervous mare.

Horse Comfort

You should also be aware of the horse's comfort. If you know that you will be going on more than one ride each day, be sure to pack an extra saddle pad or blanket. In dry, arid mountain air, sweat-soaked pads dry out fairly quickly, but in the humid South or even the Midwest, they tend to retain moisture. Your horse will appreciate a dry pad for that afternoon jaunt.

Take a Compass

A compass can benefit both horse and rider. When in the mountains, I am a firm advocate of sticking to the trails. It is foolhardy to head off through unknown, rugged country. The same is true in most trail-riding areas. There are a couple of good reasons for this. Foremost is the matter of safety. Going brush-popping in mountainous terrain is fraught with danger. Secondly, we are often riding in a fragile environment. Striking off and creating new trails in delicate areas might cause damage that will last for years. The trails are placed in certain areas for a purpose, and you should stick to them.

However, even when you stay on the trails, you can still become turned around without a compass.

Getting Lost

We were trail riding and camping in the Beartooth Mountains of Montana in our early, inexperienced days. We were careful to stay on the trails, but that didn't prevent us from having a problem. For some inexplicable reason, no one in the group had a compass.

We came to a junction in the trail. There was no sign to indicate the trail to lead us to a certain lake that was our destination. The map we had was confusing. There were heavy clouds in the sky, so checking the sun for direction wasn't an option.

We talked it over and decided that we should take a particular fork. On we rode and rode and rode and rode, climbing higher all the while. Doggedly, we stuck to the trail until we were up above the timber line. By then the trail was getting narrower and more faint.

Still, we kept on and when we came to a point where the trail began to descend the mountain, we realized what we had done. Our goal had been to follow along the river, then hang a right, go over the mountain range and drop into a valley on the other side where we would find our lake.

We had climbed the mountain, but instead of crossing over it we had followed along its crest and the trail was leading us back to our starting point. We had taken a right turn all right, but we had taken it before we got to the proper junction. We spent nine hours in the saddle that day and wound up at night very near the place we had camped the previous evening.

You should always have compass along so that when you come to junctions that are unmarked — and a great many of them have no signs to tell you which way to go — you will have a valid indicator of the direction you should head. You should also make certain you have a map you can read and understand.

Water Bucket

You need certain basic equipment to feed grain and provide water for the horses during a weekend trip. You should use equipment that is least apt to cause injury to the horse. For example, what is your water bucket made of? Are you carrying an old metal bucket with a metal bail or carrying handle? Dangerous. A horse might paw at the pail of water placed before it at night, catch a foot between bucket and bail, and frighten itself when the bucket remains attached.

Use plastic or rubber buckets.

A rubber or plastic bucket is best. If it is to be left in front of the horse for a period of time, remove the bail. You can always pack an extra bucket with a bail to carry water from its source to the horse.

Feeding Equipment

How about the feed pan? Metal pans can cause puncture wounds if they tear or bend. The best, in my opinion, are crushable rubber pans. If a horse steps on the side of the pan, it simply folds down.

Camp Stove

When on a weekend outing, we also pack a two-burner propane stove, both for convenience in making early morning coffee and in case the campsite is devoid of wood. It is also our practice, however, to pile some firewood into the pickup so that we can enjoy evening campfires. If the weekend camping spot is a popular one, all available firewood will likely have been used by previous campers. A word of caution here: Know what the fire danger is before you light

a campfire. If conditions are tinder dry, the forestry or park service personnel in charge may have decreed that no fires are allowed, which is another good reason to have a small camping stove. Of course, if you have a motor home or a live-in trailer, the stove will be a part of the kitchen fixtures.

If you are traveling with this type of rig, it is a good idea to check ahead as to electrical outlets

Basic cooking equipment.

and waste-disposal hookups. Some campgrounds don't have them. Most will have restroom facilities of some sort.

Fire Starters

A big help when starting a fire in damp conditions is a commercial fire starter, which can be purchased in any sporting goods store. Fire starters are chemically treated to burn under any condition and produce a very hot flame. They are indispensable when a rain shower has soaked the campground's wood supply or your own.

You should also make certain that matches are packed in waterproof containers. You may not need these at the campground, but in the unlikely event that you get lost and can't find your way to camp, they can mean the difference between sitting by a warm fire and sleeping in the cold.

Proper Utensils

You should also be sure to have the necessary eating and cooking utensils. It is pretty discouraging to have pancakes on the morning menu and discover that no one packed a spatula.

The best approach for us is to have one set of utensils used for nothing but camping, be it a weekend outing or a two-week affair. Linda has designed a handy utensil carrier made of heavy cloth. There are compartments for knives, forks, spoons, the spatula, and other heavier pieces. When everything is in its place, the carrying unit is rolled up and tied together with an attached string. Everything is where it can be quickly located, and it takes up very little space.

Linda has also designed what amounts to a refrigerated pannier that works wonders in preserving perishable items. She lines the sides, ends, and cover of a hard pannier with cut-to-size pieces of wall insulation. Into that pannier goes all of the frozen meat. It is topped with a chunk of dry ice. The combination of insulation, frozen items, and dry ice will preserve perishable food for several days. This piece of equipment would be something you would be more apt to use on a mountain trip, but it also works very well when tenting it for a weekend without refrigeration.

A word of caution: Near the end of the trip if anything seems to be spoiling, don't take any chances. Discard it.

Clothing

When it comes to clothing, my recommendation is think "cold" and "wet." If you are prepared for inclement weather but don't experience any, so much the better. However, if you have forgotten a raincoat and run into a downpour, you will be miserable and may become ill. In addition to the usual underwear and socks, you should pack or wear a warm vest, warm gloves, a heavy jacket, long underwear, and rubbers for your boots.

Even when it doesn't rain, there often is heavy dew on the grass in the early morning hours. If you are out tending to the horses before the sun dries the ground and grass, you can wind up with soaked feet that might make you miserable for hours. A pair of light rubbers or overshoes will prevent that problem.

Toiletry Items

A number of toiletry items can make the trip more pleasant, such as lip balm to prevent chapping and sunscreen to prevent wind and sun burns. You should also take your own soap, washcloths, and towels. The soap should be biodegradable so that it doesn't pollute or cause harm to streams or lakes in cases where waste water at the campsite eventually makes its way to these water sources.

If the campground you are going to doesn't have showers, buy or make shower bags to take with you. They are constructed of heavy black plastic with a tube running from one end. They are filled with water early in the day and then placed in the sun. The black plastic absorbs the sun's rays and warms the water. The bag can then be placed in a tree or suspended from a high spot in a horse trailer's stall so you can take a shower. Even more sophisticated solar energy bag showers are on the market today.

Eating Utensils

When it comes to eating utensils, there are some options. If you don't want to do dishes, pack paper plates. We prefer eating off metal plates and with metal forks, knives, and spoons, but we have to wash dishes after each meal.

Highly important for cooking is a pair of welder's gloves, or the equivalent, to handle hot pots and pans when you are cooking over an open fire. A pair of these gloves saves scorched fingers and hands. Welder's gloves are great because they also protect the wrists from heat and sparks.

Saddlebags

Saddlebags are more important on a mountain trip than on a weekend foray. However, if we plan to be away from camp all day, they are highly important. We use them to carry snack foods, water or soda, cameras, and perhaps field glasses for studying wildlife. They also are great for carrying along an extra sweater or jacket in case the weather turns cold.

A manufacturer in Boulder, Colorado, designed the saddlebags we use for both weekend riding and mountain trips. They are spacious and compartmentalized with a snap-on plastic tarp that makes them waterproof. If we pack them with nothing but clothes and toiletry items, they do not overly burden the horse.

Cleaning Up

As campers, we always try to leave our camping area as clean as we found it. This means cleaning up manure and depositing all other paper or metal waste products in a trash container. If there is no trash container, or if it happens to be full, take your garbage home with you.

You should take along a rake, a shovel, and a muck bucket to clean up animal waste and convey it to the proper disposal site.

Saddlebags for essentials.

You don't have to worry about manure that is spread along the trail by moving horses. Normally, it is scattered and nature will break it down. However, at a camp there is a much greater quantity in a concentrated area.

Emergency Needs

Finally, you should not forget about human emergency needs. Your supplies should include a first aid kit. You should assemble it with the thought that accidents can happen and you should be prepared for them. Many campgrounds are located a long way from a doctor's office or hospital. If you know a doctor or nurse, discuss the camping trip with them and ask for suggestions.

You should also discuss the special needs of anyone in the group. Diabetics, for example, should make certain they have an extra supply of insulin.

Persons suffering from high blood pressure should be aware that high altitude can exacerbate the condition. In fact, people with any special medical problems should consult their doctors before setting out on a camping trip in the wilds.

The first-aid kit should contain such routine items as aspirin or other inflammation fighters and painkillers; a variety of Band-Aids and non-adhesive bandages; wound and burn ointments; and perhaps even material for fashioning a temporary splint in case of a broken bone. You can obtain easily packed inflatable splints.

All members of the group should also be versed in basic life-saving techniques, such as the Heimlich maneuver and mouth-to-mouth resuscitation.

The List

Following is a general list of supplies to take on a trail ride or camping trip far from the comforts of home:

- Compass
- Map of the area, showing trails
- A cell phone
- Telephone number of a nearby veterinary clinic
- Telephone number of nearest hospital
- Clothing for both warm and cold weather, with extras of everything in case one set gets wet
- Hat
- Rain coat or slicker
- Rubbers or overshoes for wet weather
- First aid kit containing Band-Aids, painkillers, wound ointment,

burn medication, and any special medical needs

- Lip balm
- Sunscreen
- Insect repellent for humans and horses
- Gloves
- Extra pair of boots
- Small tool with wire-cutting capability
- Waterproof matches
- Flashlight
- Cooking utensils
- Cooler or insulated pannier and plenty of ice for refrigerated foods
- Heat-proof cooking gloves
- Iodized pills or purifying equipment to render water drinkable if necessary
- Camp chairs
- A tent if camping overnight
- Air mattress if you are tenting
- Warm sleeping bag if you are tenting
- Propane stove if you are tenting
- Biodegradable soap
- "Shower bag" if showers aren't available
- Camera and the auxiliary equipment it requires, such as batteries and film
- Field glasses to study wildlife
- Saddle
- Bridle
- Halter
- Saddlebags
- Extra halters and lead ropes
- Horse blankets
- Extra saddlepads or blankets
- Hobbles or picketing equipment if horses are permitted to graze
- Extra horseshoes, nails, and hammer, or an EasyBoot
- Sharp knife

- Collapsible buckets and feedpans for horses
- Grooming caddy filled with brushes, hoof picks, and curry combs
- Hay
- Grain
- Shovel
- Rake
- Muck bucket to carry manure and waste to disposal site when cleaning trailer
- A pleasant outlook and a positive attitude

14

EQUINE FIRST AID

E quine first aid on the trail goes beyond just having a first-aid kit along. Not only must you know how to use what's in it, but you also must know your horse so well that you can immediately recognize a problem that will require first aid. This is easy when the horse strikes a leg against a sharp rock or is slashed with barbed wire. One glance reveals the problem. Internal problems aren't so easy to recognize. Knowing when the horse is in the very beginning stages of colic, for example, can help get a jump on solving the problem.

Understanding Symptoms

I can't stress too much the importance of observing a trail horse when it is not being ridden. It also benefits to know the horse's normal heart and respiration rates and temperature and to maintain a record of them. Only then can you determine what is normal at rest for that particular horse, and, consequently, what is abnormal behavior or appearance.

For example, do you know the normal heart rate for your horse? Temperature? Respiration rate? Endurance racers and competitive trail riders must know these parameters well to monitor the condition and well-being of their horses during competition. We, as trail riders, should know them equally well and for the same reason, even though we aren't in competition. We should know how well the horse recovers from exertion. We can only learn this by checking the horse frequently both while it is at rest and after it has exerted itself.

Checking Respiration

Equine respiration rates vary a good deal, but as a rule a horse will have a respiration rate between twelve and twenty-one breaths per minute. A highly conditioned horse may have fewer than twelve. Watch the healthy horse as he breathes. Sometimes the respiration rate is uneven, as though the horse temporarily holds its breath. But actually it is only pausing before inhaling or exhaling. It only pauses in its breating when it is healthy and feeling good.

When the horse is not feeling well, the rate will jump to thirty to fifty or more breaths per minute and rarely will there be a pause in respiration.

One way to check respiration rate is to watch the horse's flanks. They move in and out with every breath. Or hold your hand near a nostril and feel the warm air as it is expelled. Once you have established respiration-rate parameters at rest, you should check the respiration rate following exertion, such as climbing a steep hill or galloping for a half-mile or more.

Check the respiration rate immediately in the wake of exertion, and then allow the horse to rest for ten minutes and check again. You are trying to determine how well and how rapidly the respiration returns to normal. The more fit the horse, the quicker the return to normal.

Heart Rate

Monitoring the heart rate is as important as monitoring the respiration rate. Determine the heart rate by taking the pulse when the horse is at rest prior to exercise, immediately after exercise, and again after at least a ten-minute rest.

The resting pulse rate for an adult, thousand-pound horse generally ranges between thirty-six and forty-eight beats per minute, with room for variations, depending on the animal's physical fitness.

The best way to take a horse's pulse is to place an index finger over the artery on the lower jaw, at the front part of the jaw muscle. I shift my finger around on that artery until I feel pulsations of blood going through, then I look at my watch and count. It is not necessary to keep counting for a full minute. Count the beats for fifteen seconds and multiply by four.

If you want to get a bit more sophisticated, purchase a stethoscope and apply it to the girth area to monitor the horse's heart rate.

Not only are you checking the beats per minute at this point, but you also should be getting a feel for whether the pulsations are strong or weak. A healthy horse has a strong pulsation with each heartbeat.

A significantly higher than normal heart

Checking the pulse rate.

rate may be an indication that the horse is ill. If, for example, the horse's heart rate has elevated to double its normal rate or more after the horse has climbed a hill and remains at that elevated rate following a ten-minute rest, you should be concerned.

Recording Temperature

Always take a horse's temperature rectally. Usually, the horse will not object to the thermometer's insertion, but we must take care that we don't lose the instrument inside the rectum. Equip the thermometer with a string and a clip that can attach to the tail hairs to prevent the thermometer from slipping inside. Leave the thermometer inserted for several minutes.

The normal average temperature for a horse at rest is 100 degrees Fahrenheit, with variances to 99 and 101 degrees. Find out what is normal for your horse by taking his temperature several times when he is at rest.

The rule of thumb concerning higher than normal temperatures is this: if the temperature reaches 103 degrees at rest, the horse is in distress; if it reaches 105, the horse is seriously ill and needs immediate veterinary attention.

Preventing Problems

Once you know the basic parameters for your horses, you should also think about ways to prevent injuries and problems on a trail ride. Injuries to feet and legs are most common to trail horses, and many of these can be prevented if you prepare — ensuring, for example, that shoes are on securely before you start — and are alert to potential problems.

At many trail-ride sites, you have no recourse but to tie your horses to the trailer. Are there any sharp, protruding edges on the trailer that can catch a tie rope or cause injury if the horse paws at them?

Making sure shoes are secure.

At other trail rides you have the option of tying to hitching rails or putting the horses in corrals. Don't just tie the horse and walk off. Check to make certain the hitching rails are strong and secure. If the rails are wobbly or the crossbar rotted, don't tie there. Also make sure that the secure tying spot you choose is high enough so that the horse won't get a foot over the rope.

If corrals are used, check to make certain no nails are protruding and that nothing sharp is on the ground.

Despite precautions, accidents and problems occur. Following is a rundown of a number of them, along with suggestions of how to cope.

Colic

One of the most worrisome conditions that can occur on a trail ride is colic. Researchers have learned a lot about colic, but much still remains a mystery. As a trail-riding horse owner, you should know your horse so well that you can sense the first onset of a bout with colic.

Again, you should start at home when everything is quiet and normal. Press an ear against the horse's flank and listen for his normal digestive or gut sounds. Do this both before and after the horse has eaten. You should hear gurgling sounds within that complicated digestive system as various enzymes and juices break down fiber and turn it into digestible content. Don't listen for these sounds on just one side of the horse. Listen on both sides because the sounds will vary from one side to the other.

Hearing no sounds in your horse's abdominal cavity is a strong indication of serious colic trouble. The same can be

Listening for gut sounds.

true if you hear severe gas sounds with silence in between. No sound at all often is a strong indication of impaction.

About this time or even before, the horse will be turning its head to look at its side and showing other signs of discomfort, such as sweating, drooping ears, a lackluster look to the eyes, and an uneasiness, stepping from one foot to another. Before long, it will be lying down and rolling. Remember that colic brings intense pain.

Colic is a complicated condition, and at its first sign you should call a veterinarian. However, at certain times and in certain places, that is easier said than done.

My suggestion is this: the next time your vet is out to the farm or you are in the office, discuss the matter. Explain that you might be faced with a colic problem when and where a veterinarian is not available and you would like to know what steps to take.

Puncture Wounds

An insidious type of wound that can occur on the trail is a puncture to the bottom of the hoof. This injury can come from objects ranging from nails to sharp rocks. The interior of a horse's hoof is a complicated maze of laminae, blood vessels, and sensitive tissue that can be quickly and severely damaged when infection sets in.

Immediate first aid for a puncture should involve cleaning the wound, then applying iodine and covering the bottom of the foot with iodine-soaked cotton and wrapping the entire foot so debris cannot enter the open wound. The equine first-aid kit should contain some disposable sponges and mild soap. It is as important to clean debris from a wound as it is to treat it.

When you are in the mountains, far from veterinary attention, treatment options are reduced for this type of injury. One option is

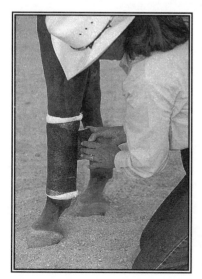

Wrapping an injured leg.

removing the metal shoe and replacing it with an EasyBoot if you must continue. The wound will be protected from contact with the ground.

Wrapping a Leg

Cotton leg wrapping is an important element in our first-aid kit. If the horse suffers an injury to the lower portion of a leg that requires bandaging, applying the cotton wrapping before using the Vet-Wrap® can help protect tendons from too much pressure.

176

Wrap an injury from the inside out and do it in layers. A leg wound, for example, would first be covered with a sterilized pad. This would be followed with several layers of gauze to help keep the pad in place. Next would come soft cotton wrapping to provide a cushion over the tendons so that they aren't compressed and injured. Finally a layer of adhesive Vet-Wrap® firmly locks everything into place.

Eye Injury

Your kit should also contain an eye-wash solution in case of eye injury, though without professional help at hand, treatment protocol is limited. Heed this warning: the solution used to wash out an eye should be only that recommended by a veterinarian, as many substances harm more than help when administered to the eye.

The best approach is to have your veterinarian demonstrate the way to wash out an eye and then mimic that procedure.

Sprains, Bruises, Abrasions

Other injuries that don't result in open wounds can occur, such as sprains, bruises, and abrasions. They are difficult to categorize because there is such a variety. However, with such injuries you can follow one treatment rule of thumb that won't get you into trouble — apply cold.

If you are in the mountains, you can use water from a nearby stream, or if you are at a campsite with running water, you might use a hose to flow water over the area. Commercial cold packs are also available. The cold water tends to prevent, or at least reduce, inflammation, and this can mean a prevention and/or an alleviation of soreness.

Sore Back

Earlier, we discussed problems that ill-fitting saddles cause. (See Chapter 12.) Suppose you discover your horse has developed a sore back during the ride. If you are riding on trails where your pickup and trailer are headquartered, you have the options of applying cold packs and allowing the horse to rest and recuperate. Although your riding might be ended for that particular weekend, you at least won't be causing your horse continued pain.

If you are in the mountains, far from the trailhead, the options are more limited. You must do all you can to alleviate the soreness, but you may not be able to rest the horse until all soreness disappears.

You may be forced to ride the horse out, sore back and all, or walk out and lead the horse. Sometimes a combination is the compromise.

An irritated area under the saddle that is in the open wound category should not have any form of powder applied to it. Instead use nitrofurazone ointment. The powder will dry out the wound and a scab will form.

It's hard to treat a sore back on the trail.

If you put the saddle back on the horse the next day, it will rub the scab off and produce additional irritation.

Rope Burn

Rope burn is an extremely painful injury, especially when a horse is either tethered or staked out. This injury usually occurs around the fetlock where the joint will be irritated with every step.

Immediately flood a severe rope burn with cold water; then gently dry the wound and apply ointment, such as nitrofurazone, from the first-aid kit. You should bandage the wound to prevent air from reaching it.

Tying-up

Tying-up, or exertional rhabdomyolysis, is a rather mysterious affliction that can have serious consequences in trail horses. To put it in layman's terms, tying-up in the horse is the equivalent to serious muscle cramps in humans following exertion.

The added dimension with tying-up in horses is that some of the muscle tissue might be damaged and compromised for the future. The horse that ties up will exhibit obvious signs of pain and will not want to walk. Heart and respiration rates likely will elevate.

Consult with your veterinarian about what to do if your horse ties up. The important thing is that you do not try to "walk the horse out of it." The horse should not be moved and should be allowed complete rest until the cramps subside.

Exhaustion

If you prepare and condition your horse properly for trail riding, you should not be faced with an exhausted animal. However, exhaustion can still occur. Sometimes age is a factor.

One year a member of our group was riding a muscular three-year-old Quarter Horse. The rider was a solidly constructed fellow, so the horse was packing a good bit of weight. However, the animal was in good physical condition and the trail not overly demanding.

Yet early that afternoon the horse demonstrated signs of exhaustion. Its head was hanging lower than it should, and it was taking short, dragging steps. We stopped at the first serious signs and decided to make camp. The rider unsaddled the horse and took it immediately to water. Because we had stopped in time, the horse suffered no damage. All it needed was rest. It was bright and ready the next morning, and we completed the ride.

The same rider still uses that horse regularly, and, with maturity, it is one of the toughest animals in our group, traveling for hours without tiring.

Dehydration

Dehydration should not occur if we are conscious of our horses' needs. Horses can become dehydrated rather quickly in the mountains just as humans can. The best prevention is to allow the horse all the water it desires at every stream crossing.

Dehydration depletes a horse's supplies of electrolytes, minerals

Checking the skin for dehydration.

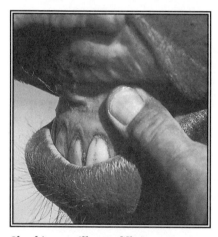

Checking capillary refill time.

such as potassium and sodium. Your first-aid kit should contain a powdered form of electrolytes that can be dissolved in the horse's drinking water to bring the animal's supply back to normal.

You can test for dehydration several ways. A basic approach is to take a pinch of skin at the neck between thumb and finger and pull it away from the body. A healthy horse's skin will usually snap back into place when released. A dehydrated horse's skin will remain slack for several moments.

You can also use the gums as a test site. Push a finger or thumb against the horse's gums, which normally are pink. When you remove the thumb or finger, the pressure spot will be white. In the normal horse the blood will rush back into the area and the pink color will immediately return. With the dehydrated horse there will be a delay in the return of normal color.

Be Prepared

Your approach to trail-riding injuries should be to do everything possible to prevent them but to be prepared with knowledge and a first-aid kit filled with the right kind of supplies to deal with whatever arises. The important thing is to discuss the trip with your veterinarian, asking for help in determining exactly what should be in the first-aid kit and how and when to use each item. The important thing is that the medications not require refrigeration as that will be nearly impossible on a long pack trip.

Giving your horse its annual series of shots or boosters before the trail-riding season begins is very important. Included are tetanus shots and immunization for sleeping sickness, rhinopneumonitis, flu, and/or other maladies that might be endemic to your particular area or where you plan to ride.

Following is a list of items that should be in your equine first aid kit:

• Wound medication
• Sterilized pads
• Rolls of gauze
• Soft cotton wrapping
• Cotton

A sampling of first-aid items.

- Rolls of Vet-Wrap®
- Scissors
- Pliers for removing a sharp object from a hoof
- Anti-inflammatory medication
- Tranquilizer medication
- Electrolytes in powdered form that can be dissolved in the horse's drinking water
- Iodine
- Eye wash solution
- Ointment to treat saddle sores and rope burn
- Disposable sponges
- Mild soap

15

PACKING INTO THE MOUNTAINS

After you have sampled a wide variety of trail rides, it might be time for something more challenging. A mountain pack trip might be your next adventure. However, it is not an adventure to be approached without some care, caution, and practice. Packing into the mountains can be a stimulating experience, but it can also be disastrous if you and your animals — especially the pack string — are not properly trained and prepared.

The easy way to go on a pack trip is to contract with an outfitter. If you take that route, the only planning required involves traveling to the outfitter's headquarters at the scheduled dates. Once you arrive, the outfitter takes care of everything. He furnishes the horse, tent, and food supplies. Usually you just furnish yourself, your clothing, and your bedroll. Some trips are so luxurious you don't even have to saddle your own horse. And, when you crawl out of your sleeping bag in the morning, coffee is ready and breakfast is being prepared.

Do It On Your Own

The harder, but more rewarding — and, I might add, more economical — way is to go it on your own. However, I must repeat that a mountain pack trip is not something to be entered into lightly. The mountains are grand and glorious, but they are unforgiving if you take them for granted and don't properly prepare yourself and your horses and/or mules.

We learned the hard way. When I think back to our first pack trip, I am still embarrassed by the miscalculations and poor judgment.

Selecting and Training a Pack Animal

One of the first requirements when preparing for a pack trip is the procurement or development of safe and sturdy pack animals. You may have the right candidates for a pack string in your own pasture or you might have to consider making a purchase.

I'd like to point out a few general things you should know about pack animals. For example, in your search, it's best to look for an animal that has already been trained to carry heavy loads. That way, even if you've never done it before, at least the animal will be familiar with his job. Then, it's up to you to learn how to pack him properly. Read books, watch videos, and take any packing and outfitting classes available through local horsemen's associations and sometimes even community colleges.

A pack trip requires good, sturdy pack animals.

It is impossible to outline all that one needs to know in a single chapter. And, even if all the information were presented, you still need hands-on experience.

If you're just starting out with packing, I suggest you purchase a pack system that doesn't require knowledge of fancy knots and rope tying. Beginner-friendly pack outfits that simply fasten with buckles are available as well as soft panniers (packing bags) that fit over regular riding saddles, so it's not necessary to purchase a packsaddle in the beginning. But as you get more into it, you'll no doubt want a packsaddle. The two traditional types are the Decker (a trade name) and the sawbuck (a type of saddle), but both take a little education to get things right. (Again, there are good books and videos on this subject. And most anyone who has done any packing will be glad to answer questions and give demonstrations.) You'll also need a set of panniers, which are available as hard boxes or soft bags made of canvas, nylon, or leather, to store the goods for your trip. Take some time to research the packing method that best suits your needs and your comfort level.

One of the greatest inventions for the beginning packer is the H-pack. It is called that because of its shape. Designed to carry the soft items, such as bedrolls, it is placed on the packsaddle after the panniers are in place. It works best with the sawbuck saddle because the H-pack wedges down between the front and rear braces. When you pass the straps of the H-pack down through the handles of the panniers and draw them up tight, you have a secure load that doesn't require ropes to hold it in place.

Packing Tips

Once you have your pack horse, it's time to get it acclimated to all the equipment.

To start, place the packsaddle on the horse and adjust it to fit properly. This means that the saddle should rest on a sturdy pad on the horse's back, with the front breast collar just snug enough that the saddle can't slide to the rear if you are ascending a steep hill. The same is true of the breeching, a heavy, thick strap that goes around the rear quarters. It shouldn't be so tight that it chafes, but it must be positioned so that the saddle and packs don't slip forward when you are on a steep decline.

Unlike a trail horse, a packhorse must get used to a tight rear cinch. To keep the packs or panniers in place, both the front and rear cinches must be drawn up snugly. Certain horses might take some time getting used to this, so be sure you get the horse acclimated before ever putting on panniers.

It's also a good idea to go on an outing or two to get the horse used to carrying just the packsaddle and being ponied. Go for a trail ride, and pony (or trail) the packhorse behind on a long lead rope. Try to pick some rather narrow trails so that the packhorse gets in the habit of following and not walking beside the lead horse. If the pack animal comes up too closely behind, check him with the lead rope that's attached to his halter and encourage him to remain in position. If the horse has been trained to yield space, this will not be a problem. A flick of the lead rope will remind him.

Get the packhorse used to carrying the packsaddle.

Once the packhorse is comfortable with the packsaddle and being ponied, you'll want to introduce him to the panniers. You can easily frighten the horse if you simply walk up and put the panniers in place on the packsaddle. Let the horse see them, feel them with his nose, and smell them before you put them in place. Once you have them on, lead the horse around awhile, petting him, and talking quietly.

As mentioned earlier, there are a variety of panniers. Some are hard-sided boxes built to conform to the animal's conformation, or spring of rib, and others are basically canvas or nylon bags. They hang down, one on each side of the horse.

If you plan to travel into grizzly bear country, you'll want at least one set of bear-proof panniers. These are designed in such a way and manufactured from such strong material that even a powerful grizzly bear can't tear them open. All edible items and toiletry items, such as toothpaste and soap, should be packed inside the bear-proof panniers.

Once your pack animal has adjusted to the packsaddle, you'll want to get him used to carrying weight. A couple of fifty-pound bags of feed that fit in each pannier are a good start. The feedbags will not make noise and will provide an evenly balanced load. Head out on trail rides near home until the packhorse is totally acclimated and accustomed to carrying a load.

As the training progresses, you can add to the load so that the pack animal gets used to carrying more weight. The rule of thumb for weight is that you don't exceed 20 percent of the animal's weight. In other words, if your horse weighs one thousand pounds, the maximum load he should carry is two hundred pounds. In my opinion, two hundred pounds of dead weight on a horse's back is substantial, and we try never to exceed it no matter what size the packhorse might be.

As the training progresses, you will want the horse to face some challenges from the load. For example, pack items that jingle or rattle in the pack so that he gets desensitized to the noise. Tie something on top that flaps in the breeze — like a piece of plastic — so that he won't panic in the mountains when something comes loose on the load.

Leading a String

Things can get a bit more complicated if you are going to lead more than one pack animal. I have seen commercial pack strings, nine and ten mules long in the mountains with only one rider up front. Of course, these animals do this day after day and don't make many mistakes.

At one point we had three mules in our pack string. I used to cause near-accidents from startled motorists in Kentucky when I'd head down the road with my horse leading three mules in a line, loaded with panniers.

You must be aware of the pecking order if you line out packhorses or mules this way. I have an excellent pack mare that will carry a heavy load over difficult terrain without missing a step. However, she will not tolerate another horse behind her. If she's in a pack string, she has to bring up the rear.

Leading a string of packhorses requires practice.

All the horses in the string must also be compatible as far as traveling speed is concerned. If you have a long-striding horse in front of a slower one, all of the animals will travel at an uneven pace.

When tying pack animals together, make certain that you have enough space so that they can travel easily, about half a horse length, but not so much they can get a front foot over the rope.

Again, it is a good idea during these early outings to have experienced riders on experienced horses accompanying you. If you are ponying three pack animals and have a problem, it can be very difficult to solve if you are alone. You can wind up with all three pack animals and the horse you're riding being tangled in the ropes holding the string together.

It is important that you have a safety valve to prevent this from happening. The safety valve should be in the form of a light cord that connects the lead rope to the packsaddle of the horse or mule in front of each individual other than the pack animal bringing up the rear. The goal, when a wreck occurs, is for the cord to break and free the trailing animal or animals and thus avoid entanglement.

Of course, you don't want the cord to be so light that it breaks from the lightest pressure. I have found that a single twine string fills the bill during practice sessions and a light rope when the pack string has become more experienced.

When practicing with the pack string, try to expose the pack animals to as many experiences as possible. Climb and descend steep hills. Cross water and pause in a stream to allow them to drink. This will help teach you about the length of lead rope between the individual animals. You want them to be able to reach the water, but you don't want them to step over the lead rope.

If you pause during your ride and allow the pack animals to graze while tied together, you are asking for trouble because it is very easy for one or the other to get a foot over the lead rope as they walk from one tuft of grass to another. Untie the rope that is connecting a pack animal to the one in front of it and hold each lead rope separately in your hands while they are grazing.

By spending a lot of time on the practice trails with your pack string, you are accomplishing several things; you are teaching them about staying in line and going over obstacles in an orderly way and you are getting them fit.

You also will be teaching yourself a bit about handling a pack string. As the person leading the pack animals, you are placing yourself in a position of responsibility when an obstacle is encountered. It is up to you to make certain that the lead pack animal doesn't rush headlong over a log, for example, and drag the rest of the string behind it. It is also your job when watering to make certain that the place you pick as a watering spot has enough room to accommodate the entire string. If it doesn't, keep on going. There'll be a better spot ahead. If there isn't, you might be faced with stopping and disconnecting the string. Then you can tie some of the pack animals to trees while the rest are being watered and then reverse the process for those that were tied.

While ponying three or more pack animals in a string is an adventure, it is best to lead only one and have other members of your riding group do the same thing. It cuts down on the potential for accidents.

It is important when ponying that the traveling speed of the horse you are riding is the same as that of the pack animal. If your riding horse is moving rapidly and the pack animal is traveling slowly, it will be a miserable trip. Conversely, you don't want the pack animal to be walking so fast that it is constantly attempting to pass the horse you are riding.

There is only one way to get it right and that is to practice until ponying a pack animal becomes second nature to you and the horse you are riding.

When you have reached that point, it is time to get serious about planning for that packing adventure.

PLANNING AND PREPARING FOR THE BIG ADVENTURE

Once you have committed to a pack trip, the preparation begins, even though it might be a year away. First of all, you must decide where you are going and obtain all possible information about the area.

A letter or phone call to the regional forestry headquarters where you plan to ride will either result in information about the trails and any available maps, or in your being directed to a district office. I have found that dealing directly with a district office is much better. I also like to talk to a forester or trail supervisor by phone because they often are the ones who are out on the trails.

I tell the park official how many will be in our group, discuss the experience level of horses and riders, and ask about a route that will bring us back to the trailhead without retracing our steps, if possible. With that as a base, I then ask the person what trails he or she would recommend for our group. I also inquire about potential campsites at various intervals along the trail.

Once you've expressed your goals and experience level, your contact person can better offer suggestions on where to go and can estimate how long it will normally take to get from one campsite to another.

Reading Maps

When you have established the basics, ask about the availability of maps. Normally, the maps are easy to read, though there are exceptions. Your best option is a topographical map, despite its larger size. These maps are marked with elevations and are color-coded. Brown areas indicate areas above the timberline with no grass; green areas mean grass is available.

Normally, dotted lines represent the riding trails. Tight zigzags of dotted lines in a brown area indicate you will be traveling above the tree line over switchbacks that take you through a mountain pass. These routes can vary from very safe to downright scary with a potential for danger. Sometimes the switchbacks are literally carved into the rock wall of a cliff, and if you are afraid of heights, they can be scary to negotiate.

The problem is that the maps don't show you just how scary a set of switchbacks might be. Just recently I was discussing a trip through a nearby mountain range with an acquaintance who knows the area well. Two trails go over different mountain passes but wind up at the same destination. When you look at them on the map, the passes seem to have the same degree of difficulty.

However, my acquaintance described one as a "wet your pants" pass and the other as an "easy" one. We opted for the "easy" one for that particular ride.

Study maps before taking your trip.

Once you have received the maps and studied them, it is time for another call to the district forestry office. First, make sure that you are reading and interpreting the maps correctly. Secondly, discuss a proposed route and ask about its feasibility. How wide is the switchbacking trail through the mountain pass? Does that narrow blue line on the map indicate a little creek that can be forded easily or is it a deep stream? Does that broad green spot along the river truly indicate a meadow of grass that will provide feed for your group of horses? What month of the year and what week or weeks during that month are the trails likely to be free of ice and snow?

Elevation Figures

You should be certain to look at the elevation figures when deciding to travel from Point A to Point B on a given day. The distance may only be nine or ten miles, but if you are traveling from a starting elevation of 6,000 feet above sea level and arriving at a destination that is 9,000 or 10,000 feet, much of that ride will be a hard uphill pull. Far different if the elevation figures show you are going from 6,000 to 6,500 feet. That ride might be only several hours long while the other one, usually involving switchbacks, may take nearly a whole day.

Grizzly Bears

Another key question to ask is whether the area you have chosen for your ride is inhabited by grizzly bears. These huge creatures are shy and normally avoid human contact, but they can be very dangerous. You will want to know if they are present in the area and what regulations you must follow to prevent contact. The district forestry office will provide detailed instructions concerning camping regulations if you are heading into griz' country.

Know the Area

It also is important to know if there are special features that might affect you and the ride. A case in point. We rode into the region around Frying Pan Lake in the Big Horn Mountains one time and camped in a picturesque spot. My son Greg was, and still is, an enthusiastic trout fisherman. The first day we camped there, he was up early, fishing along the creek that meandered through the area. Later that day he thought he would try his luck on the other side. We thought nothing of it as he could cross the river by stepping on exposed rocks.

He returned later that afternoon, soaked and shaken. Unknown to us, that was the day scheduled for water to be released from Cloud Peak Reservoir. It had headed down creek with a rush. When Greg tried to return to camp, the rocks he had crossed earlier were covered with swirling water roaring downstream, and the creek was getting deeper by the moment. Fearful that he was going to be stranded on the wrong side, he plunged into the water and struggled across.

Bad Weather

Another experience on the same trip brought home another lesson on the necessity of being prepared. When you are in the mountains, be ready for all kinds of weather. A sunny, warm day may end with snow and falling temperatures.

Before you set out make sure you know where you are going.

We were following a circuitous route that would ultimately return us to the trailhead. As we left Frying Pan Lake, we headed up a high slope known as Ant Hill. On the upward climb it began to mist. Soon mist turned to rain. We donned slickers. Higher and higher we climbed. Soon we were battling not only rain, but also fog. Then came the snow.

As we neared the summit, visibility became so poor that we could see only a short distance ahead. This posed a serious problem because we were above the tree line and the trail was basically invisible. The forest rangers had marked it with cairns, piles of rocks, placed at various intervals. No problem when it wasn't snowing or foggy. However, the visibility was such that we couldn't see from one pile of rocks to the next.

We devised a safety plan. When we reached a pile of rocks, one rider would remain there, while the rest of us moved forward, spreading out but keeping each other in sight. When we located the next pile of rocks, the finder would let out a shout; we'd all gather there for a moment and then repeat the process. Slowly and laboriously, we worked our way up and over the summit. Never have trees and a clearly visible trail looked so good as when we had descended to that point on the mountain's far side where the weather pattern reversed itself.

Snow turned to rain. Rain turned to mist, and, eventually, we rode out of it all together.

The good news is that we had prepared for the possibility of changing weather by carrying warm garments and slickers. When you are riding in the mountains, dress in layers. If it becomes warm, simply remove a layer; if it gets cold, add one.

Plan a Year Ahead

If you decide to pack into the mountains on your own, begin planning and preparing for the adventure a full year in advance. Find out if any of your acquaintances happen to be experienced mountain riders. If you find someone who is, don't be bashful. Ask a million questions. True mountain riders will be delighted to offer advice and share experiences.

Decide where you want to go and then learn everything you can about the area.

When you contact the district forestry headquarters for maps, also ask for rules and regulations governing horseback pack trips. They will send you a packet that lists rules for everything from how close to a stream or lake you are permitted to camp to the number of "beating hearts" permitted on the trip. There are areas where the maximum number of beating hearts for a group is twenty-five. A beating heart includes any person or animal.

Some national forests require a horse permit before you can enter. The permit doesn't cost anything, but it must be filled out before beginning the pack trip. It will ask when you are entering the forest, when you are leaving, and where you plan to camp. It is the forestry service's way of keeping a handle on trail usage and to know where to look for you in an emergency.

Hay Rules

Many national forests also have rules about bringing in hay. In some areas, even when camping at a trailhead, you must feed only

hay that is certified as being free of all weed seeds. It is a good idea to get your trail horses accustomed to eating alfalfa cubes before heading on a trip. They are easier to pack and, because of the heating process when they are prepared, most cubes are weed-free and meet forestry requirements. Don't take this for granted, however; find out about weed-free regu-

Know the hay rules in advance. lations.

Health Rules

Also find out about equine health rules and regulations, which vary from state to state. If you are traveling with your horses to Montana, for instance, your vet must call the Montana Livestock Board and obtain a permit number for you. All states require a negative Coggins test result, but there are state-by-state variations as to how long a negative test is valid. Some states also require a health certificate issued no more than thirty days prior to entering the state.

Equine health rules can vary.

Each state has its own livestock board, and officials there have a list of all other livestock boards in the country. Find out from your state board or vet whom to call or write about health rules and regulations.

Brand Inspection

If you live in a western state, you must be aware of the brand inspection laws. If you live in Wyoming, you need valid brand inspection papers in hand to haul your horse from one county to another legally.

We learned the hard way about some of these rules. In our early years of traveling west, we had spent a delightful week camping in the Beartooths and laid over that night at the Billings, Montana, fairgrounds. A race meet and a fair provided plenty of fun activity.

After a pleasant evening we loaded our horses the next morning and headed east. We had gone only a short way when a highway patrolman pulled us over. He wanted to see our papers. We pulled them out. He gave them a glance and wanted to see our permit number. What permit number? We didn't know we needed one. He informed us that we did.

The reason we had been stopped was that two horses had been reported stolen from the fairgrounds the night before and every trailer heading away from Billings was being treated with suspicion.

He instructed us to remain parked along the highway while he radioed for a brand inspector to come check us out and to decide whether our horses should be impounded. Our pleasant trip was rapidly losing its luster.

Two lucky breaks came our way. The patrolman was informed by radio that the two missing horses had been found. They hadn't been stolen but had gotten out of their stalls and were wandering around the fairgrounds. The second was that he couldn't locate a brand inspector. Not knowing quite what to do, he told us to go on home.

From then on, we have been diligent about having all paperwork in order when we cross state lines.

The List

Once you have your destination in mind and have set about procuring all the necessary information, think about your equipment, such as packsaddles, tents, sleeping bags, cooking and eating utensils, and, it seems, a million other things.

Make another list that includes these steps:

1. Obtain maps.

2. Discuss trails with a district ranger and find out the best time of year for your ride.

3. Check out equine health regulations in states on your route and at your destination.

4. Take inventory of riding and packing equipment.

5. After inventory, carefully check each piece of equipment and replace anything that is worn or weak.

6. Give attention to camping gear, especially the tent. Is it in good

repair? You don't want to discover a tear in the roof during a mountain rainstorm.

7. Check on capacity of saddlebags. Are they large enough to carry your changes of clothing?

8. Check on cooking utensils and cooking grates or stove. Are they of a size that will fit into the panniers? You don't want to be packing the night before a trip and find out the pans or grates are too large.

9. Plan a conditioning program for your horse that will begin in early spring and then stick to it.

10. Discuss the food menu with other members of the group. Is anyone allergic to any particular food? Are there certain foods that some members simply can't or won't eat?

11. If fishing is on the agenda, check with the district ranger concerning regulations. Can you buy a five-day out-of-state license, for example?

12. Check out fishing equipment. It is difficult to transport long fly rods or even casting rods into the mountains. Look into the possibility of collapsible rods that are only about eighteen inches long when pushed together.

13. Take a good look at warm-weather clothing. Most important here is a warm raincoat. Beware of the heavy plastic variety. They trap too much body moisture.

14. Carefully check saddlepads. Is the inner surface becoming crusted with dirt and hair. A thorough cleaning may be needed, or else the purchase of a new pad may be in order.

15. Thoroughly check the towing vehicle and trailer. Pack the trailer's wheel bearings with grease and check out flooring, wiring, tires, and hitch.

As you think and plan the trip, the above list likely will expand. The key is to jot down anything that comes into mind that should be done and then to check it off when completed.

As part of your horse's conditioning program, you will want the animal shod. It is a good idea to reset shoes one week before you leave. This allows some recovery time if a shoe has been poorly fitted.

By now, you should have a saddle and pad that fit your horse and a bridle and bit that he wears comfortably. As mentioned earlier, during the winter is a good time to check billets, cinches, and stirrup leathers for wear. One man that accompanied us on some of our early excursions only rode a couple times a year and paid little attention to his equipment. For him a ride in the mountains was an opportunity to fish for trout.

We were climbing out of a deep valley one day when the billet holding his cinch broke. The horse was rounding a slight turn in the trail at the time and the saddle slipped around the horse's barrel, with the rider hitting the ground with a crash beneath the animal's belly. Fortunately, the horse stood quietly while the dazed fellow crawled clear.

A check of the broken billet revealed that it was dry and cracked with age and neglect. The rider escaped injury, and we were able to do some repair work that allowed him to saddle up and ride again, but it could have been a serious accident.

Routine cleanings and applications of saddle soap do wonders for the life of leather.

Packing Equipment

The equipment for the packhorses is as important as that for the saddle horses. Unfortunately, new equipment is not cheap. However, if you plan to make numerous trips into the mountains, good pack saddles and panniers are worthy investments. If you aren't sure mountain riding and packing are going to be your cup of tea, you would do well to consider using packs that fit over a western saddle. They are much cheaper and carry a load quite well. There are openings that fit over pommel and cantle, with two spacious bags on either side.

Bear in mind when you are using this type of pack equipment, a packed horse is carrying dead weight, and the western saddle is apt to slip forward or backward as the horse ascends and descends steep slopes. Therefore, you might also have to use a breeching or crupper to keep the saddle in place. If you spend the winter talking, planning, and preparing for the trip, your appetite for the adventure will be duly whetted when spring rolls around.

Oxygen Supply

Many people worry that horses coming from near sea level will have trouble acclimating to the mountain altitudes. If they are physically fit, horses have an easier time adjusting than humans, and it's all due to physiology. Red blood cells distribute oxygen throughout the body. The horse is unique in that it stores extra red blood cells in the spleen. When the normal supply circulating through the bloodstream is being used to the maximum, the spleen contracts and pushes forth more blood cells to serve as additional oxygen carriers.

You will find upon reaching altitudes of 8,000 feet and above that you will be gasping for air with any little exertion until you have become acclimated, yet your horse will recover quickly even after a long, steep climb. You don't have that extra supply of red blood cells to carry additional loads of oxygen.

Just as your animals should be well conditioned, so should you. Traveling through rugged terrain puts a whole lot more stress on legs and the rest of your body than riding along a trail with only gentle hills and valleys.

Doing some cross-country walking or jogging (on your own feet) before heading off on a mountain trip is a good idea. Talk with your doctor before beginning an exercise program so you will know what is right for your body.

Forestry Offices

Following are addresses and phone numbers of U.S. Department of Agriculture regional forestry offices from which information can be obtained. Folks at these offices may not have all of the specific information you need, but they will be able to refer you to a district headquarters that will.

Northern Region
Federal Building
200 East Broadway
P.O. Box 7669
Missoula, MT 59807
406-329-3511

Rocky Mountain Region
740 Simms St.
Golden, CO 80401
303-275-5350

Southwestern Region
Federal Building
333 Broadway SE
Albuquerque, NM 87102
505-842-3292

Intermountain Region
Federal Building
324 25th St.
Ogden, UT 84401
801-625-5306

Pacific Southwest Region
1323 Club Drive
Vallejo, CA 94592
707-562-8737

Pacific Northwest Region
333 SW First Avenue
P.O. Box 3623
Portland, OR 97208
503-808-2468

Southern Region
1720 Peachtree Rd NW
Atlanta, GA 30309
404-347-4177

Eastern Region
626 East Wisconsin Avenue
Milwaukee, WI 53202
414-297-3600

Alaska Region
Federal Office Building
709 West Ninth St.
P.O. Box 21628
Juneau, AK 99802
907-586-8806

PACKING UP

You've made the plans, studied the maps for the zillionth time, checked the equipment for the hundredth, and conditioned the horses. The trip is about to begin, and now it is time to pack equipment and food for the big adventure.

Before you begin, however, you must answer this question: How many packhorses do you need?

Do you decide how much gear you want to take and then determine the number of packhorses needed to carry it? Or, do you determine how many packhorses you have and then take the amount of gear they can comfortably carry? As mentioned earlier, the rule of thumb is that the amount of weight in a pack should not exceed 20 percent of the horse's weight.

We normally have three packhorses or mules for the five or six members of our group. The number of riders varies year by year but never exceeds ten. The larger the number, the more Spartan the meals unless we are able to camp near trout-filled streams or lakes. Two of the pack animals carry hard-sided panniers, topped by a strapped-down H-pack, and one carries a set of soft canvas panniers.

Many people travel with much larger pack strings. I know of one group of eleven that took a trip into the mountains and had one packhorse per person plus another four to carry extras. The "extras" consisted mostly of beer and other beverages.

The problem with that many animals is that you limit yourself as to campsites. It takes a lot of grass to provide forage for twenty or more animals.

All the Comforts

Another friend who enjoys packing into the mountains with a small group generally figures one packhorse per rider. He likes all the comforts of home, such as a collapsible table for eating, a wood-burning cook stove, and a spacious tent.

We get along without a table, pack in only a small propane stove, and use nylon tents that can be rolled into small, tight packages. We have warm sleeping bags that can also be rolled into small, tight packages. Our saddlebags are roomy and compartmentalized. Each person carries a change of clothing in them. The key here is that clothing is generally light and, thus, the saddlebags are not an undue burden for the horse.

It is different when I join another small group of friends for elk hunting. Then, we pack in a large wall tent; a wood-burning stove; a larger, but warmer sleeping bag; and heavier clothing. With all this baggage, we wind up with a minimum of one pack animal per person.

A Matter of Economics

The problem with needing a large string of pack animals is that they can be expensive to own or to rent. In many parts of the country, the cost to rent packhorses can start at forty dollars per horse per day. Owning a number of extra horses used only once or twice a year as pack animals is not economically feasible. Additional pack animals also means additional packsaddles and panniers. Again, this equipment is not cheap.

We have tried to strike a sort of compromise by owning our pack animals and equipment, but keeping the numbers to a minimum. Also, our packhorses and pack mules double as riding mounts.

Packing Saddlebags

Pack your saddlebags first. These will carry an extra set of clean outer clothes, undergarments, and clean socks. They will also contain a toothbrush, toothpaste, lip balm, and other toiletry items, plus any necessary medications.

The saddlebags should also contain a washcloth and towel, plus a bar of biodegradable soap, as well as some additional warm clothing, such as a sweatshirt and long johns.

As you pack the saddlebags, visualize how you will use each item. You'll probably want to put on clean socks and underclothes each day, so pack them in a separate compartment where they are easily reached. Your clean outer clothes won't be needed for a day or two, so pack them on the bottom.

A small flashlight, loaded with fresh batteries, should be at the top in the saddlebags. Each person should have a flashlight.

Rain Gear

Above all, don't forget a raincoat or slicker. This can be rolled tightly and tied behind the saddle.

Your saddle must have long leather thongs behind the cantle to tie the slicker and saddlebags firmly in place. Our trail-riding saddles are handmade, and we have asked the saddle makers to put extra-long leather thongs behind the cantle.

By now, your group has decided on the menu, and someone has

Rain gear is essential.

made a mammoth grocery shopping trip. The next task is to get all the foodstuff inside the panniers. Before you pack the food, think about when each meal is to be served.

Refrigerated Pannier

One of our panniers is insulated with building insulation and does a good job of keeping food frozen for several days if you cover the top with dry ice.

Consider the food that goes in the refrigerated pannier before packing. For example, if you are going to serve chicken, pack it on top. Thawed chicken spoils very quickly. So if chicken is on the menu, be sure that it is prepared one of the first nights in camp or even at the trailhead the night before leaving.

To cut down the "thaw time," the refrigerator pannier should be the last one packed; in fact, it is wise to pack it only moments before heading off for the drive to the trailhead.

A number of meat items don't require refrigeration. You can buy canned chicken, canned hams, beef stew, and a variety of other canned or cured products.

The same is true of bacon. We have discovered that you can buy canned bacon that needs no refrigeration. The variety we discov-

ered, processed in Hungary, is found on the food shelves in places like K-Mart. It is heavily laden with salt and preservatives, however, and wouldn't be appropriate for those on a salt-free diet.

When planning our mountain meals, we generally schedule the meat thusly — chicken first, pork next, and, finally, beef.

Securing a pannier.

Once the refrigerator pannier is packed to capacity with frozen products and topped with dry ice, it should be opened only when food is removed. You should also immediately place it in the shade when you reach the campsite.

Our record for frozen-food preservation is five days. On one occasion we packed steaks in the bottom of the refrigerator pannier for our meal the last night in camp. When we took them out, they had thawed but remained icy cold. We cooked the steaks over hot coals, and they were delicious.

However, be very careful with meat of any kind that has been frozen and then thawed. If there are any signs of spoilage, seal the meat inside a garbage bag and pack it out. Food poisoning can wreck a fun trip in a big hurry.

Weight

One of the first considerations when packing animals is weight, whether dealing with saddlebags, the refrigerator pannier, or the panniers carrying tents and sleeping bags. You should never exceed the 20 percent level with packhorses, and you want to keep the saddlebags as light as possible on your riding horse.

Balance is just as important as weight. Each pannier must weigh the same amount. If it doesn't, the packsaddle could tilt, and one of the panniers could wind up under the animal's belly. In addition, uneven weight can irritate a pack animal's back in a hurry. It also is important that the load be compact and not so high as to be unwieldy.

Don't overburden the pack animal or your horse.

When packing, use a scale to monitor how much weight you are loading in the panniers. Special scales just for this purpose are on the market and are not expensive. This type of scale is easy to pack and use. You merely run a strong rope between the pannier handles, attach the scale hook, and lift. Of course, a pannier weighing 100 pounds may require inserting a bar or strong stick through the top hook on the scale and the efforts of two people to hoist the pannier off the ground.

The hard panniers will contain the canned meat, fruit, and vegetables, plus packages of dried food. Unlike with the refrigerated pannier, packing by meals will be more difficult because you will want the heavier cans of goods on the bottom.

Limited Space

You will be working with a limited amount of space, so make every square inch count. As an important space-saving measure, one of the first things you should do is remove all dried food from its container, providing the food itself is inside a sealed bag. Boxes are bulky and relatively unyielding; sealed packages are more malleable and space conserving. And, if a package of dried pasta or potato flakes gets a little squished, it really doesn't matter all that much.

We like fresh eggs for breakfast, but packing them can get a little tricky. One of the best ways is to leave them in the carton and then put a light layer of cushion material around the carton. Or, purchase plastic egg cartons, which work very well. You also can remove the eggs from their shells and place them in a plastic container.

You should also try to get at least some of the cooking and eating utensils inside the hard panniers. The danger of putting them inside a soft canvas pannier is that they can gouge the pack animal in the side as it walks.

After a few tries you will become adept at putting one cooking utensil inside the other and also filling each empty space with a package or can of food. The coffee pot, for instance, can be stuffed to the brim with food items.

Usually, we wind up packing some of the cooking equipment inside the soft panniers. To protect the pack animal, we place air mattresses or sleeping bags on the side that comes into contact with the horse's body and put the utensils on the outside of the pannier.

Our picket lines and pins, plus extra rope, lead lines, and extra halters also go inside the soft panniers.

The H-Pack

One of the most valuable pieces of packing equipment is the H-pack, so called because it is shaped like a capital H. It is designed to go on top of hard panniers but can also be used with a number of soft panniers. Inside it we place our nylon tents, more of the sleeping gear, and other odds and ends.

The beauty of this piece of equipment is that it fits atop the hard panniers, and because of its construction, settles firmly in place over the sawbuck. It straps

The H-Pack goes atop the panniers.

down tightly to the hard pannier handles. Thus, we have a secure pack that needs no ropes or special methods of tying. If you treat the H-pack with additional waterproofing material, it will do a good job of shedding rain.

Of course, if you want to be sure that everything is kept dry, each pack should be covered with a well-secured, waterproof tarp.

For us, the H-pack has pretty much replaced the use of ropes and hitches to hold the load securely. It might not be the way of the true old-time packers, but it is simple, fast, and easy to secure.

At least one person in the group should have a list of each pannier's contents. That may seem unnecessary when packing at home, but if you have four panniers sitting in a row at a campsite, it might be tough to remember which one contains the coffee.

Three Important Items

Three other very important items to pack are a shovel, an axe, and a saw. All three should be of the short-handled variety. The saw we carry can be disassembled quickly and easily, the pieces fitting together in a compact metal case slipped inside a pannier or tied on top. The shovel has a fold-back blade that makes it even shorter, and the axe has a very short handle.

Before strapping down the lid of the hard panniers, we slip the handle of the shovel under the straps on one and the axe under the lid straps on the other pannier. This locks them firmly in place, and because they are short, they don't protrude to either the front or rear of the pannier.

The axe and saw are used to cut up firewood or, in some cases, to cut through a deadfall on the trail. The shovel is our prime "bathroom" equipment. It is used to dig a small hole to bury individual human waste. We do not dig a big toilet pit as this can be destructive to the environment.

We now come to the question of self-protection, especially when riding and camping in bear country. We make certain that one member of the group has a firearm, but it is packed primarily in case a horse has to be put down.

Pepper Spray

The best protection from bears, besides a clean camp that doesn't attract them, is a can of pepper spray. We make certain that a can of pepper spray is in each tent. We also insist that anyone leaving the campsite to go fishing takes a can of pepper spray.

Riding and camping in the mountains, we have seen grizzly bears and black bears, but we have never had one attack. These animals are very shy and normally don't seek human contact. They are only a problem if surprised or if they have learned that a camping group means food because someone has left scraps and garbage behind.

You will rarely see a bear while riding because bears have keen hearing and will drift out of sight when they hear approaching riders.

Other Areas

The previous packing information has dealt heavily with taking a pack trip into the mountains because we have done the bulk of our riding, camping, and fishing there. However, mountains aren't the only place to ride and camp. All across the country, from the deserts of Arizona to the forested regions of the eastern United States, there are publicly owned areas where trail riding and camping are permitted.

Each has its attractions, and each provides special concerns that require advance preparation. Know about the region where you are going to ride and pack accordingly.

For example, if you are going to ride through desert country, you should be very concerned about finding water at campsites. And, while grizzly bears might not be in the desert, other harmful creatures and insects certainly are. Learn about them in advance.

Each area has its attractions.

If you are planning to ride in forested areas of the Midwest or East in the summer, you must be aware of potential problems with wood ticks and deer ticks. Deer ticks often carry bacteria that cause Lyme disease in humans and horses.

Adding Enjoyment

Learning about flora and fauna adds another dimension to the adventure, so include a pocket guide to the area's plants and wildlife.

Seasons vary according to altitude. In Kentucky, for example, spring flowers make their appearance as early as February. High in the western mountains, spring might not arrive until early July. There are few things more beautiful than riding through a huge meadow of wildflowers. That experience is enhanced if you have a pocket guide to help you identify them and tell you when they bloom.

The same is true of wildlife. The animals you see will vary region by region and a pocket guide can help identify them. The neat thing is that you never know what or when you will see wildlife.

One of our more dramatic experiences occurred in the mountains of Colorado. We were winding down a mountainside toward an open valley when we heard elk bugling. We came to an opening in the wooded trail and below us was a herd of several hundred elk on the move. We hadn't frightened them. They were merely traveling quietly along a trail in the valley below. We simply sat quietly and watched until they disappeared into a patch of timber.

While I wouldn't classify our group as bird watchers, we are very much aware of the different species and use another pocket guide to help identify them.

While we don't pack in a guide to weather patterns, it can help in our enjoyment if we have at least packed into our minds information about cloud formations and the type of weather fronts that are apt to move through the mountains.

I will share one more magnificent, stirring experience. We were camped in the Beartooths at about 10,000 feet. A thunderstorm rolled in. However, we were so high that the clouds had rolled in below us. The sky above was clear. It was an awesome experience to stand on a mountain top and look down on clouds that were pouring rain at a lower elevation. We could see streaks of lightning cutting through the tops of the clouds and thunder rumbled up from down below.

This was one moment we didn't need a pocket guide to enhance our enjoyment.

18

RIDING THE HIGH COUNTRY

You are finally ready to hit the road. If reaching your trail-riding destination will take longer than a day, you should already have made arrangements for a layover. If possible, plan the trip so you arrive at the layover in daylight. Unloading a group of horses in the dark at a strange location invites trouble.

Even more important, arrive at the trailhead in daylight. This is often easier said than done. Some trailheads are miles off the main highway, over a torturous, winding road, climbing higher and higher.

An example is a campground trailhead in Wyoming's Wind River Mountains. It is thirty miles from the main highway, but it takes an hour and a half to traverse that distance when you are pulling a horse trailer. When obtaining information about the trail you plan to ride, also ask about the road into the trailhead.

Start in the Morning

When you arrive at the trailhead and a lot of daylight remains, you might be tempted to load right up and start riding. This generally isn't a good idea. You should wait until you have an entire day ahead of you. It is better to spend the remaining hours of daylight getting everything organized for the next morning. This is a time to study the map some more so that you know approximately how long it will take to get to your first campsite.

That first day it is far better to have only a short ride rather than a

Ride when you have the entire day ahead of you.

long one. Here again, getting information from the forestry folks well before your trip is a must. However, you must be certain that you have correctly interpreted the information. You may have been told that it is an easy ride from the trailhead to the first camping spot. And, so it might be — for someone who has spent a lifetime in the mountains. Everything is relative. An easy trail for someone used to the terrain may be daunting to your group. This is the reason it is extremely important that when you contact forestry service personnel you make clear the group's experience level and the kind of terrain in which you and your group normally ride when not in the mountains.

Saddle Up

One of the basic tasks on the ride-in morning is to get all of the riding horses and pack animals saddled and ready. This includes the task of placing the panniers on the pack animals. This is not a one-person job. We usually make it a three-person job, with one person holding the pack animal in a clear area rather than tying it to a hitching rail or trailer. The person putting on the first pannier remains beside the animal, not letting the weight come to bear, while the second person does the same from the other side. Then each allows the pannier to settle into place so that the weight settles evenly on the pack animal. The panniers should have been weighed beforehand to make sure they are evenly balanced. Even a pound or two can make a difference.

Trailheads and Wrecks

For some reason trailheads seem to be the site of most wrecks — someone's horse spooking or bucking or a pack slipping off. One reason might be that the horses and mules have had little or no exercise and are bursting with energy. The key is not being in a hurry. If needed, exercise horses and mules a bit before tying on saddlebags or lashing down panniers.

Establish a pre-arranged formation.

Do the inexperienced riders in the group a favor by double-checking their equipment to make certain they have properly secured their saddlebags and firmly tied their slicker or raincoat.

The trail leader should also decide at this point what the riding order will be. Often mountain trails permit only single-file riding, so you should establish a pre-arranged formation. Anyone riding a fast-walking horse should be close to the front. Those riding slower horses should be toward the end of the line.

Commercial outfitters usually have the pack string travel separately so as not to hinder the progress of the riders. With a private group that usually isn't an option. What works best for us is to have the riders ponying the pack animals lead the way. Our reasoning is that if something is going awry usually it will involve one of the packs. By having the pack animals up front, everyone behind them is aware if a pack needs adjusting or whatever, and the pack string is never left behind to fend for itself. We also think the pack string should set the pace.

Ponying a pack animal properly is its own art form. First of all, you don't tie the pack animal hard and fast to the saddlehorn. Any pause that the pack animal makes in that situation may result in its being severely jerked forward. When you are leading a packhorse or mule, you should carry the lead rope coiled in one hand. Then, for example, if you come to a stream or muddy spot and the pack animal pauses for a better look before crossing, you can simply play out some of the coiled rope and halt your leading horse rather than unceremoniously dragging the pack animal through the spot in question.

Rest and Watering Stops

When you are resting at a mountain meadow, all the animals usually drop their heads and graze. Whether or not you are ponying a pack animal, you should dismount, giving your riding horse relief from your weight and allowing you to maintain better control of the pack animal. If you stay on your horse and play out lead line so the pack animal can graze, either the horse you are aboard or the pack animal might become tangled in the lead rope.

Stopping at watering spots in the mountains, especially streams, requires a bit of thought and coordination if you are to get the job accomplished without incident. Seeing a watering spot ahead, the lead rider should pass the word down the line that the entire group will water there. This is a signal for everyone to halt when the group reaches the water.

The leader should ride into the water with whatever pack animals are being ponied. The riders behind can do likewise as long as there is no crowding. Once the first group has finished drinking, the horses should go to the opposite bank and stop. If the first group rides out of sight, the horses left behind might become agitated and refuse to drink. If the river is broad, the lead rider and whoever enters the river at that time should ride to the far bank before stopping, allowing other horses on the near bank to enter the river and drink.

Remember that all horses don't drink water at the same rate. One horse might gulp it in while others will sip very slowly and daintily. Whatever the case, each horse should be allowed to drink its fill before moving on.

Stopping for water takes planning.

If you arrive at a somewhat questionable river crossing, it is wise to reconnoiter before leading the group into it. My usual approach is to hand over whatever pack animals I am leading to someone else while I ride alone into the river on my trusted lead horse. Unencumbered, we can thoroughly scout it out before the entire group enters the water. In this type of situation, the trail leader must have a horse that will move forward steadily but very carefully.

If the bank of a crossing appears unduly muddy, you might even want to check it out on foot before committing a horse. At times like these, well-trained trail horses are vital. They should be prepared to stand quietly on the trail during delays and not be spinning about, getting nervous and fidgety.

Downed Trees

You can also encounter delays when you come to trees across the trail. Though a forestry service trail crew might have gone through and cleared all obstacles a week or two before, one night of high winds might have downed other trees.

You should have a saw and an axe packed in a handy manner.

217

These are must-have tools when you have to clear blowdowns that can't be negotiated or bypassed.

The lead horse is the key animal in the group in these situations, as well as in setting the pace. This horse should be a true trail-riding veteran. You don't want it to move forward in foolhardy fashion, but you want it to trust its rider, negotiate new obstacles without hesitation, and set a comfortable pace.

A lead horse balking at every new obstacle causes confusion and concern all down the ranks. Soon a tangled mess of riders and pack animals develops.

The person riding the lead horse should be capable of quickly making a decision and acting on it. Arriving at an obstacle, the lead rider should decide whether to go over or around it — or whether to stop and consider other options, such as chopping a pathway. The less time spent debating the issue, the better.

Know the Trail

When you are planning a mountain trip, it is essential to check thoroughly on the trails. We didn't check out a trail in advance in the Bob Marshall Wilderness in Montana one time, and the result was a grueling ride. We had studied the map and decided we would ride to a small lake, camp overnight, and ride back the next day on a different trail. Our topographical map showed the lake where we planned to camp in a green area, indicating forage for the horses and mules. Had we checked, a forester would have told us that the green was a marshy area along the shores of the lake. There was no edible grass.

Also, had we checked, we would have found out that the trail was not being maintained that particular summer, though it had been in the past. We battled our way over downed trees, sometimes electing to go over them and sometimes being forced to fight our way through heavy undergrowth to get around them. Finally, weary from the hard ride, we arrived at the little lake with no proper place to camp and no forage for the horses.

Our only option was to ride back down on another trail. Fortunately, that trail was well-maintained. Nevertheless, we arrived at a camping spot bone tired, with darkness setting in.

Leading the Horse

I have been asked several times whether I would recommend getting off and leading a horse on a narrow, switchback trail with a steep drop-off on one side. It is a difficult question to answer, but normally I would say no. Horses are sure-footed creatures, and they don't want to fall off a cliff any more than you do. They have four legs to keep them on that trail and even an inexperienced horse will generally do a good job of this.

The problem with leading the horse is that if you stumble, the horse may inadvertently step on you. On only one occasion did I suggest that everyone dismount and lead horses down a trail, and I think that was a mistake. We were taking a new trail back to the trailhead and came to a spot where it dipped over a rim and dropped steeply into a valley. It angled down but with no protective switchbacks.

I feared that one of the middle or rear horses might lose footing and cause a chain reaction. We dismounted and began leading them down. The horses handled the trail with sure-footed ease, but one group member stumbled and fell. This startled his horse, and it headed down the trail without him. Fortunately, the horse didn't step on him.

If you do feel you must walk through a dangerous area, take a very firm grip on the reins, no more than two feet from the bit. That way you can use the reins and bit as a brake if the horse should surge ahead. If you are walking at the end of the reins, the horse can be on top of you before you have a chance to stop it. If there is a drop-off on one side, pick a path next to the cliff wall, just in case something spooks the horse. If the trail is narrow and the horse gets between you and the cliff wall, there is a danger that you could be pushed over the edge. For this reason it is very important to have trained your horse to be led from either side.

The bottom line, however, is that horses almost never fall from steep, narrow trails unless we ask them to negotiate those trails under snowy, icy, or slippery conditions.

The Arabian gelding that I used as a lead horse for some years had the disconcerting habit of looking at scenery below when we crossed high mountain passes. He would always cock his head toward the drop-off and enjoy the view. This produced the sensation, when sitting on his back, that his body was going to follow his head and he was going to walk right off the trail. Early in his career I think I made dents in his side with my outside leg, trying to make certain he was aware that walking off the trail wasn't an option. Eventually, I adjusted to his idiosyncrasy and could at least relax when riding such trails.

Afraid of Heights

Some people are afraid of heights. If the fear is profound, they perhaps should not be riding in the mountains. If the fear is more on the mild side, it can be counteracted by not looking down. One of my favorite recollections involves taking Linda's aunt, Marilyn, over Jordan Pass in the Beartooths for the first time. I had her ride behind me so that I could reassure her when we got to a short but

Acrophobics shouldn't look down.

scary section of the trail with a straight down drop-off on one side.

As we started along this portion of the trail, I began talking to her without turning my head. "Just look straight ahead," I told her soothingly, "and remember, you are riding Ferd. He is about the safest trail horse we own. I guarantee that he won't miss a step and..."

Marilyn, or Moy as she is known affectionately in our trail-riding group, interrupted my "soothing" chatter with an exclamation. I turned in the saddle, and there she was leaning to the side and looking over the edge. "Les," she said, all excited, "there's an eagle flying below us." So much for my alleviating her fears.

Campsite

I have been told that pilots of small planes are always conscious of the possible need for an emergency landing. They routinely and perhaps even subconsciously scan the ground for a smooth, level area, just in case they are forced to make a landing. The lead rider should be doing the same relative to potential campsites, even though your group should have chosen a spot for camping in advance. Problems necessitating an early stop can occur.

I have already recounted the story of the three-year-old horse that became very leg weary when we were only about three-fourths of the distance to our planned camping area in the Bridger-Tetons. We were in grizzly bear country so finding a suitable camp was a must. We needed a spot with tall trees so that we could hoist our panniers out of reach of bears, and, of course, we needed water and forage for the horses. A couple of us had noted that a short way back we had passed a nice meadow along the river, so the whole group did an about-face and returned to it to set up camp.

Look for level ground.

Finding an appropriate camping spot in the mountains is not always easy. The first concern is for the horses. They need both a water and feed supply. We don't pack grain, hay, or cubes, so we depend on finding adequate grazing areas. This is another reason to discuss the trail in advance with someone who knows, such as personnel at the district ranger's office. There often are only limited areas along a given trail where grass and water are available. You should know where they are before beginning the trek.

Sitting the Saddle

How to sit the saddle properly in mountainous terrain is a subject for some debate. Some advocate standing in the stirrups and leaning far forward when climbing a steep slope and leaning far back when descending. I don't feel that either of those approaches is correct. The important thing is to stay in balance with your horse. I have found what works best is to consider you and the horse to be an inverted T. The horse is the cross mark on the upside down T, and you are the long mark. If you maintain a relatively straight-line position with that cross mark, you will usually be in balance with the horse's center of gravity. However, this might mean leaning back slightly in the saddle when you are going down a steep slope and inclining your body at a slight forward angle when going uphill. However, exaggerated changes of position can get you out of sync with your horse.

Meeting on the Trail

Though you might want to believe that you are all alone with your group in the wilderness, it will not be true. More and more people are taking to the mountains as backpackers and horseback riders, and it is likely that your group will run into some of them.

The rule of the road is for those riders heading down to give way to those going up. However, there is only one rule that should be followed and that is to use common sense, with a good measure of courtesy thrown in. If you are heading upward and see a group descending toward you, immediately look around and determine whether it might be easier for your group to get off the trail and let the other riders pass.

Above all, smile and be pleasant. You are in the mountains for enjoyment, not confrontation.

Meeting hikers is also inevitable. The rule of the road is for hikers to step off on the trail's downward side and let horses pass. The reason for this is quite simple. A person on foot can step off the trail, into what might be uncertain footing, more easily than a group of horses.

This, too, is no place for confrontation. If the hikers hesitate in giving way, simply stop and sit quietly. Again, smile and engage the hikers in conversation. This does two things. It makes for a pleasant situation, and your horse, when it hears a voice coming from that odd-looking figure on the trail with the humpbacked look, will know that it is indeed a human and not some creature to be feared. Plus, it provides the hiker an opportunity to assess the situation and, hopefully, decide to step off the trail. If need be, explain in a calm voice that you have a group behind you and that if all of them are forced to leave the trail, an accident might happen and that members of the hiking group could be inadvertently injured in the process. Besides, you might add, riding off the trail damages the environment.

It has become popular in some areas for hikers to use llamas to carry their camping equipment. We have met a few on the trail and, for some reason, the sight of llamas seems to strike fear into the hearts of many horses. If you see llamas approaching, be on guard.

On casual riding jaunts around home, you will probably have found some shortcuts between trails. Avoid taking a shortcut in the mountains, particularly when traversing switchbacks. Switchbacks serve two purposes. First, they make for a safer trail. Instead of climbing straight up or descending straight down, the curving back and forth of the trail makes it easier for horses to maintain footing and eases the stress of the climb. Second, the switchbacks help curtail erosion. A well-worn trail that heads straight down a mountainside will soon become a deeply rutted gully from rain and snow melt. Stay on the trail.

First Campsite

Finally, you have arrived at the campsite. Hopefully, it is all that you had envisioned — a grassy meadow for the horses, a stream or

Take care of the horses first.

lake for water, and smooth, level ground for setting up tents, plus a magnificent view.

The animals that deserve your first attention when arriving at a camping spot are the pack animals. They have been carrying dead weight all day and deserve to be unloaded first. Unloading should follow the same procedure as loading, with one person on each side to remove or support a pannier in such a way that the animal isn't standing there with heavy weight hanging from one side and nothing on the other.

19

MOUNTAIN CAMPING
Leaving No Traces

Select a tent site on hard ground and at least 200 feet from any rivers or streams and the trail itself. This type of spot isn't always easy to find in the mountains, especially with a large group. This is the reason you should contact forestry personnel familiar with the area before your trip.

Set up your camp among trees rather than out in an open meadow where vegetation will be trampled and where the wind has a clean sweep at tents. Of course, there is the remote chance that during an electrical storm, lightning might strike a tree near the tent. However, a greater risk would be to have your tent, with its metal support rods, be the highest object in an open meadow.

When you first arrive at the campsite, tie riding horses and pack animals to trees until you unload your gear and set up a high picket line. Make sure the tree is at least eight inches in diameter to assure it's sturdy enough if the horses pull back. At that size a tree is also less likely to sustain bark damage than a smaller, younger sapling.

Feeding the Horses

Once you've unloaded the gear and unsaddled the animals, it's time to let them eat. This means driving picket pins or putting hobbles on the horses so they can graze. We don't let all of the hobbled horses eat at the same time. As mentioned earlier, we have learned the hard way that horses can leave camp in a hurry even when hobbled.

Horses can graze in shifts.

Horses that get along well should graze together. They will already have an established pecking order. The same can be said for the horses that are tied while the others graze. If you tie only one horse, for example, it inevitably will become agitated by being left alone and will start pawing. If one of the horses is a bit excitable, tie the calmest one in the group beside it to serve as a security blanket.

Horses eat a lot of little meals because their stomachs are small and can hold only a limited amount of forage. An hour or two of grazing at a time is about all that is required to fill an equine stomach.

When ground-picketing to graze, make certain that each horse has sufficient space so it won't get entangled in another's picket ropes. When you see grazing horses nibbling at a tuft of grass here and another there, all the while moving about, it is time to tie them to your now-established picket line. Then allow the horses that were tied to do their grazing.

Watering

Once the horses are finished grazing, they should be watered. Exercise caution when you are watering at a new spot. Make certain the bank area is firm. When camping, you have the luxury of time, so locate a good watering spot on foot.

Above all, don't have horses skidding down banks to get to the water. This will cause long-lasting environmental damage. It is a good idea to pack a collapsible pail. With it you can always get water for the horses and avoid damaging the stream bank.

Picket Line

Your picket line or lines between trees should be equipped with knot-saver devices threaded through the picket rope. Once in place, the knot saver devices won't slide back and forth along the line. You should allow enough space for each horse so that it can make a 360-degree turn without bumping into a horse on either side of it. This likely will require more than one picket line. To hold the picket line to the tree, use a belt several inches wide that won't cut into the bark of the tree. These are available at most tack shops.

Because the knot savers are removable, you can make use of lash ropes — the ropes used to hold a tarp in place over the packs — as picket ropes, thus cutting down on bulk in the form of additional ropes.

Environmental Damage

Environmental damage should be avoided when you are pitching tents. At one nice camping area Linda and I were very disappointed to find that previous visitors had dug a little drainage ditch around their tent. The result was a scar that will be there for years to come. Pick a spot that has natural drainage so the soil doesn't have to be disturbed.

Always pitch the tents a safe distance from the campfire. Falling sparks can quickly burn a hole in a nylon tent roof or wall. Plus, if you are in grizzly bear country, you will want to cook well away from where you'll be sleeping.

Your camping goal should be to leave no trace. Every campsite should be cleaner when you leave than when you arrived.

Care for Equipment

Once you have tents set up and sleeping gear laid out, it is time to take care of your riding equipment. We spread saddle pads and blankets to dry in the sun as soon as we remove them from the horses. Once dried, they can serve as secondary mattresses under the sleeping bag if you don't mind the smell of horse sweat. Using them in that manner also protects against rodents that might chew on them for the residual salt if they are left outside.

There are a couple of ways to protect saddles. One is to run a log between two trees. Place the saddles on the log and then cover the saddles with a tarp. However, with this method a strong wind accompanying a rainstorm can send the tarp flying into the forest.

The method that works best for us is to take along some large garbage bags. Simply fold stirrups and cinches inward, stand the saddle on its front end, and stuff the bridle down into the hollow between the two skirts. Then, pull the garbage bag down over the whole thing. Make sure the pommel area is resting on the end edges of the garbage bag, and you will have a saddle protector that will withstand both wind and rain.

We also pack a lightweight tarp that we stretch between trees to form a canopy over the cooking area. This is invaluable when we are preparing a meal in rain.

Fresh Drinking Water

You should prepare the water supply for the group soon after arrival. Drinking directly from streams and lakes is an invitation to illness because of bacteria that are present, even in swift-moving streams. There are several ways to purify water. You can use a small pump that purifies the water as it passes through. It is a bit laborious and time-consuming but very effective. Or you can use iodine tablets; however, some people have expressed concern that water purified with this method might not be the best for the body. Or, you can simply boil the water and let it cool.

Once we have purified water, we pour it into a plastic container and hang it in a tree. Dehydration is always a concern when you are in the mountains, so make sure there is plenty of drinkable water on hand both in camp and on the trail. Each rider should carry a canteen of water when riding.

Firewood

Another immediate need when you arrive at camp is firewood. In some areas it is available in abundance. In heavily used areas it might be very scarce, another good reason for packing in a small camp stove.

The rule of thumb for gathering wood is to pick up only that lying free on the ground or dead branches on a tree. Chopping down a green tree provides very poor firewood at best and leaves a scar.

Building a Fire

If there is an established fire ring at the site, use it. The soil already has been damaged and using an existing ring will not damage a new area. If not, use a fireproof ground cloth or construct a sand mound on which to build the fire. These will protect the ground from intense heat, which may kill off any future vegetation.

When building a fire, we jokingly challenge the fire builder to a "one match" effort with natural ingredients. More often than not this doesn't work. However, a little nest of dry pine needles and twigs will ignite easily. If, however, the wood is damp from an earlier rain, you might want to resort to a commercial

Take precautions in building a fire.

229

fire starter. Fire starters can be procured at any outdoor sporting goods store and work very well.

We make certain that we pack along several butane cigarette lighters, even though we don't smoke — just in case all of the matches get wet.

Waste Disposal

Another indispensable camping tool is the shovel. Camping in the woods gives going to the bathroom a whole new meaning. The best way to dispose of human waste is to make a cat-hole, about six inches deep, back in the woods — well away from camp. When you have finished using it, cover it with the earth and sod that have been peeled back, and Mother Nature will do the rest in breaking down and absorbing the waste.

Bathing and Cleaning

Nothing is more important in the mountains than a clean, bountiful water supply, and it should be protected. Never take a bath with soap and shampoo in a stream or lake. Use only biodegradable soap in camp and never use it in the water supply itself.

Have a pan of water and a bar of soap near camp for washing hands and face, and when the water becomes dirty, dump it well away from the tents and cooking area and refill the pan. The rule is that whoever dumps the pan refills it from the nearby lake or stream. As mentioned earlier, if you want to be sophisticated, you can carry in your own shower. A black plastic bag, specially designed to absorb heat from the sun's rays, complete with a hose and shower spigot, can provide warm water for a shower, provided that you let the filled bag rest in sunlight for several hours.

Garbage Bag

One of the first things to do after getting tents up and a fire going is to set out a garbage bag. Everything burnable should be burned; everything else should go into the garbage bag. You keep the garbage bag from becoming bulky by crushing all cans before placing them in the bag.

The ironclad rule should be this: "If you can pack it in full, you can pack it out empty."

Bear Country

How you handle food and other odor-producing items while in camp depends on whether you are in bear country. In grizzly country specific regulations govern handling food and toiletry items. These items either must be stored in bear-proof containers or hoisted into a tree so the container holding them is ten feet off the ground and at least four feet from the tree trunk.

In some areas with a large grizzly bear population, forestry service employees put up "food poles" at specific camping spots. These are long poles hung between two trees. You simply tie a rope to the pannier handles, toss the free end over the pole and hoist the pannier aloft. A few sites may

Bear-proof containers are hoisted high.

even have metal bear-proof containers waiting for you. However, don't plan on having either the food pole or containers when you are in bear country. Be prepared to find a suitable tree or trees where you can hoist your food supply ten feet into the air.

Bear-resistant panniers are now on the market. They have screw-down lids and are made of a durable synthetic material that even a grizzly can't destroy. They are expensive, but we have purchased a set for our food. If your food is stored in bear-resistant panniers, you can forego hanging them in a tree. However, as an additional safety measure, all food should be stored a minimum of one hundred feet from any tent and the cooking fire should be at least that far from any tent.

Even if you aren't in grizzly country, you should abide by the above rules. Black bears, which inhabit almost all of the western mountain ranges, can also be camp marauders.

As mentioned earlier, when in bear country, at least several members of the group should be equipped with canisters of pepper spray. A blast of pepper spray in the bear's face and eyes is a much better deterrent than a .30-06 rifle. Grizzly bears can be very hard to kill even when hit in a vital area. Pepper spray won't kill, but the burning sensation generally causes the bear to leave the area. The canisters can be fastened to your belt and thus readily accessed.

Tidy Camp

If you are fortunate and take the right precautions, you will not have to use the pepper spray. This means keeping a neat and tidy camp.

Remember this ironclad rule: Never take panniers of food, bear-resistant or not, into your tent.

We broke that rule once, and I still remember the incident vividly. And, I might add, these were not bear-resistant panniers. Fortunately, it was only a scare, but the incident made a profound impression on me.

It was one of several trips on which I was the only male. All of the other male partners had opted out for one reason or another. There were five of us in the group, Linda; our dear friend Betsy; Linda's aunt, Moy; and Judy, who was recovering from cancer.

We got to our campsite later than planned. By the time we had finished with the evening meal, it was getting dark. Food items in our panniers were in a helter-skelter state. Judy was exhausted and ready for bed. She suggested that we leave everything until morning and straighten it out then. She also said to close the pannier lids and set them in her tent. There was plenty of room because she was tenting alone.

For some unknown reason we all agreed even though we knew better. Our only excuse, and it is a mighty thin one, is that we were in country that was reported to be free of bears. No matter. It was the wrong decision.

I started thinking about it as I crawled into my sleeping bag. I knew we shouldn't have put the food panniers in Judy's tent. But, she was sound asleep and needed her rest. I drifted off to a fitful sleep.

About 2:30 a.m. I sat up straight in my bedroll. Wide awake, I listened. There it was again, the sound of a bear's claws ripping through the wall of Judy's tent. Clad only in my shorts and tee shirt, I shot out of the sleeping bag, grabbing my pistol with one hand and flashlight with the other. I bolted out of the tent door like a knight of old, ready to take the field of battle, slay the dragon, and rescue the damsel in distress.

I swung the light toward Judy's tent. Caught in the glare, eyes opened wide, one front foot raised was a yearling deer. It was standing on a small piece of plastic that had escaped a pannier. Apparently, we were camping in what was something of a deer gathering spot and this one was amusing itself by using its sharp, cloven hooves to make scraping noises on the plastic.

By now everyone had been awakened by my crashing about. We rescued the panniers and took proper care of them. I slept well the rest of the night. That was the first, last, and only time that cardinal rule has ever been broken in our camp.

Poor Campsite

While a lot of decisions can't be made by committee, the selection of a campsite often should be agreed upon by everyone in the group. If even one member of the group is totally unhappy with the site, it will rub off on the rest.

I would be remiss if I did not pass on one other story about this same five-member group that involves just such a decision. The four women had humored me the day before the incident that follows by stopping at one of my favorite trout-fishing lakes. We camped there for the night even though there wasn't much forage for the horses.

It was a long, slow trip down the mountain the next day. My pack

mare decided she hadn't had enough to eat and was snatching at everything in sight, even though sometimes she had to balance precariously on the edge of a switchback. As mentioned in the training chapter, that is a habit that shouldn't be tolerated. However, this was our endurance racing mare, who had a mind of her own and was in the category of "you can't teach an old dog

All riders should be happy with the campsite.

new tricks." When she was hungry, she ate. It was as simple as that.

By the time we got down the mountain to the river valley, my arm hurt as the result of the jerking that followed each of her stops, my back was sore, and my humor was sour. It was a bit early in the day, but I decided that was enough. We would stop and camp. The women weren't all that keen on the spot I selected but again decided to humor me, or so I thought.

They headed off into some trees back from the river to look for a spot to pitch tents. I had found a fire ring for the cooking and campfire. I was busy getting panniers down and my horse unsaddled, grumbling to myself because I wasn't getting any help.

Unknown to me, the four women were having a council of war. Something had happened that made them determined not to camp at this spot. Linda decided that she shouldn't break the news to me because she was my wife and I might brush off her suggestion to keep going (not true). They settled on Betsy, who is like a little sister to me. She also has a mischievous streak. They knew that when Betsy went into her "sweet little sister" mode, I wouldn't refuse whatever she might ask (true). I was still in a bad mood, getting equipment organized, when I realized Betsy was standing beside me.

"Les," she said solemnly, "we can't camp here."

"And why not?" I asked.

"Because there are snakes in that tree."

"Snakes? You're kidding me."

"I wouldn't kid you."

"Yes, you would."

"Well, this time I'm not. Come see for yourself."

I walked a few paces with her. Sure enough, there were a bunch of baby snakes wriggling around the roots and even into the lower branches of a tree. They appeared to be harmless little garter snakes.

I knew I was whipped.

"Okay," I said gruffly, "better get your horses saddled."

She smiled sweetly at me. "We haven't unsaddled."

A Night's Rest

When all the chores of the day are finished and the campfire is burning low, it is time to crawl into that sleeping bag for a good night's rest. Be sure your flashlight is at hand in case one of the horses should break free. If you are in bear country, make sure that a can of pepper spray is just inside the door of each tent.

If you are new to the high country, don't be surprised if you don't sleep soundly all through the night. First of all, there will be all sorts of strange sounds. Second, there is the matter of your body becoming acclimated to the thinner air. When we lived near-sea level and traveled to the mountains, I always needed one night to acclimate. I'd wake up gasping for air as my respiration rate slowed to a point where not enough oxygen was being supplied. A couple of deep breaths and back to sleep I'd go, only to awaken again an hour or two later. After a day and a night in the mountains I'd be acclimated and would sleep soundly. Now that we live at an altitude of 5,500 feet, the problem never occurs, but it does afflict others who come from lower elevations to ride and camp with us.

Leave the campsite clean.

Leaving It Clean

The important thing when it comes time to break camp is to leave it clean. You want the next arrivals to wonder when last the camp was used, whether they arrive a few hours or a few days later.

Piles of manure should be scattered with a shovel. And, when you leave camp, make absolutely sure the fire is out. Pour copious quantities of water on it and then scatter the ashes.

20

COOKING IN THE MOUNTAINS

I love cooking over an open fire on trail rides and do so at every opportunity. We pack in at least one, and often two, lightweight grills to make it easier to do so. They slip down inside a pannier and take up very little space. When unfolded, they stand on four metal legs that keep the cooking surface above the fire.

Getting the hang of open-fire cooking takes trial and error. Most beginners make the mistake of cooking over a too-hot fire. Normally, licking flames indicate the fire is too hot for much of anything except boiling water and making coffee.

When building a cooking fire, pick small but very dry branches and allow them to burn down to glowing coals. When the flames are gone but the coals are radiating strong heat, it is time to cook. The secret to success here is timing. You should prepare all your ingredients while the fire is blazing away and get them on the moment the coals reach optimum temperature.

Cookware

Our chief cooking utensil is an elongated lightweight pan fitted with a cover that also serves as a frying pan. The pan itself is very light and has two handles for easy handling.

It's tough to keep track of hotpads on a camping trip. One pair of heat-resistant gloves is better because they are easy to pack and find. They also protect the wrist and even the upper arm from intense heat

Use heat-resistant gloves.

and flying sparks. Metal handles on everything from a coffee pot to cooking pans become extremely hot over an open fire. Also helpful are long-handled forks and tongs for turning and handling the cooking food.

Carrying Capacity

The type of food you take in depends on your carrying capacity. During some of our very early treks, we took nothing but packaged, dehydrated food. This is an efficient way to take food, and there are many varieties, some of which are very tasty. Also, since this type of food is usually in sealed paper or plastic containers, there is little waste material such as cans or other containers. For most dehydrated food, you merely add water, stir, heat, and eat.

Augmenting meals of this type with fresh-caught fish is more than adequate for many campers.

Others don't mind packing canned food in and out for their meals. This fare can range from beef stew to chicken and dumplings.

Comfort Zone

Meal preparation should always be within the group's comfort zone. Talk about what food the members like and don't like beforehand. Get everyone involved with recipes and planning. If no one likes cooking over a campfire or camp stove, keep it simple. If, on the other hand, everyone looks on eating and meal preparation as an adventure, let your imaginations fly.

We are in the latter category. We love good food and see no reason why we should be bereft of it when we are riding in the mountains.

Others in our trail-riding and packing groups are of the same bent, so we are constantly experimenting and exploring this culinary world.

We often pack in frozen meat. Making this possible is the aforementioned "refrigerator" pannier that Linda designed. The important thing is to pack the pannier properly. Food that is most apt to spoil quickly in case of thawing, such as chicken, should be packed on top with pork next in line and beef on the bottom.

It is also important that you keep the refrigerator pannier out of the sun at all times while you are in camp. By using the special pannier, we have enjoyed meals ranging from simple casseroles to roast leg of lamb.

I recall one incident before we were making use of the refrigerator pannier. We were camping on a mountain lake and a couple of the women in our group had combined efforts to make a superb chicken-and-dumpling dish with canned and dehydrated foods. We ate to the point of bursting, and still there was much left over. Camped

Gathering around the open fire is a highlight.

239

quite close to us were two young cowboys and their dog. They worked for a rancher and were checking for cattle in the general area.

Our two kind-hearted cooks decided to share our bounty with these poor young chaps who probably had nothing but a can of beans for their supper. The two ladies dutifully trekked on foot to the other camp, only to find the young men were dining on T-bone steaks, with one still sizzling on the grill for their dog. They said they were cooking all of the steak they had left because they feared it would spoil.

The cowboys respectfully thanked their visitors for the kindness and generosity but turned down the chicken and dumplings.

Two Meals

We normally eat only two meals when mountain riding and camping — breakfast or brunch and dinner. In between, we pack along snacks like granola bars and Moy's special "gorp" mixture of dried fruit, a variety of nuts, and M&Ms. Sometimes we also have dried beef jerky in our pockets to chew on as we ride.

How early we eat breakfast depends on the day's plans. If we are going to remain in camp and do some fishing, it might be a leisurely brunch. If we are heading out to a new campsite, it will be an earlier quick breakfast.

Campfire biscuits.

When we have time, our breakfasts often are hearty affairs. For riders who want only a light breakfast, there are options. Flavored oatmeal dishes, for example, require adding only hot water. Some of these are really tasty and nutritious. We use them a lot when getting up well before dawn in elk-hunting camp.

Use dried fruit to keep breakfast balanced. It takes up very little space and is tasty and nutritious. We also pack in little individual-sized cans of peaches and mixed fruit. They come with an easily opened lid — just pull the tab.

As I mentioned, we generally eat only two meals a day, but we do pack in bread, canned meat, and cheese for sandwiches in case somebody gets hungry during the day or we arrive at camp too late to cook an evening meal. Bagels make an excellent replacement for bread because they stay fresh longer and are durable.

Whatever the meal, try to use as few cooking utensils as possible. You have only so much room on the grate. That doesn't mean there isn't room for imagination, especially when dinner or supper — depending on where you're from — is involved. It can be as simple as a hamburger-helper hot dish or as sophisticated as leg of lamb.

Our crowning achievement was just that — seasoned leg of lamb prepared over an open fire at 10,000 feet. We prepared an oven of sorts from aluminum foil and then maintained steady heat from a bed of coals. A surprise mountain hailstorm in the midst of the cooking added a bit of a challenge. However, when the meal was served, the group unanimously declared it to be excellent.

Of course, positive comments on the cook's skills are to be expected. Criticizing camp cooking is something to avoid. Our close friend and ranching partner, Chuck Hales, maintains that there are two people on a camping trip that you never criticize — the trail leader and the camp cook. One, he says, can get you lost and the other might quit feeding you.

Most of our campfire recipes originated in a cookbook or were passed down through the family. Through the years we have changed and modified them until they fit our particular needs.

If you aren't into open-air cooking or don't have the pannier space to pack that type of food, plenty of options are still available, ranging from complete meals of dehydrated food to the old standbys of tuna helper, instant potato flakes, and a variety of dehydrated soups and stews. In many instances all you need to do is add water and heat.

I don't recommend one hunting buddy's approach to dining. When left to his devices, a meal might consist of a can of chili with the lid only partially removed. That way he can hold the can over the fire with pliers until the chili is hot. The only utensil that gets dirty is the spoon he uses to eat the chili directly from the can. It works for him.

You will be burning up a fair amount of energy in gathering wood, saddling horses, and hiking off to prime fishing spots at high altitudes, so nutritious food should be high on your list. How imaginative you want to be in its preparation is a personal thing.

As you grow in experience, you likely will become more adventuresome. Here are some recipes that we enjoy. They range from breakfasts to dinners:

Eggs in a Nest

I won't get too specific on quantities. Everything should be geared to the number of persons in the group and their appetites.

1. Rehydrate a package or two of dehydrated hash-brown potatoes.

2. Cut bacon into small pieces and fry (one or two of the canned variety). It should be fried to at least the medium level of crispness or a little beyond.

3. Set the bacon aside and remove a portion of the grease.

4. Sauté a chopped onion or two in the bacon grease until soft but not yellow or blackened.

5. Add the potatoes to the onions, cooking them until the potatoes are brown and crispy. You might need to add some of the reserved bacon grease to keep the potatoes from sticking to the bottom of the pan.

6. When the potatoes have been properly browned, stir in the pieces of bacon. Spread the mixture of potatoes, bacon, and onions evenly over the bottom of the pan and use a large spoon to make a series of indentations (nests) in the potatoes.

7. Carefully crack and pour one egg into each indentation. Add a little salt and pepper to taste. Cover the pan. To facilitate the cooking of the eggs, you might shovel some hot coals on top of the cover.

8. Pour yourself another cup of coffee and sit back and wait for the eggs to cook, checking them occasionally by carefully removing the cover with heat-resistant gloves.

9. When the eggs have reached the desired degree of firmness, serve with a spatula, being careful to keep each "nest" intact. Simply slide the spatula under the nest, lift, and place it on a plate.

10. Enjoy.

(To cut down on fat, remove all of the grease after frying the bacon and replace it with light cooking oil.)

Free-For-All Breakfast

Often in trail-riding groups, someone won't like this or can't eat that. Turn breakfast into something of a smorgasbord that can accommodate them.

The ingredients are flour tortillas, eggs, breakfast sausage, green pepper, onions, tomatoes, canned salsa, shredded cheddar cheese in a sealed packet, sour cream, and mushrooms.

1. Fry the desired quantity of sausage.

2. Remove the sausage from the pan. Set aside and sauté the mushrooms. If they are fresh, sauté until they have reached that magical point where they are firm to the teeth and filled with maximum flavor. If they are canned mushrooms, merely warm them through.

3. Break into a pan the number of eggs that will feed your group. Beat the eggs thoroughly.

4. With some grease from the sausage — or vegetable oil — to keep the eggs from burning, add the eggs, the sausage, and the mushrooms to the cooking pan and scramble.

5. Finely chop some green peppers, onions, and fresh tomatoes. Put each ingredient, including the shredded cheddar cheese, on separate plates. Set out the canned salsa and the sour cream.

6. Use the cover of your pan to warm the flour tortillas to the point where they are soft and easily rolled.

7. The diners can build their own breakfast by first placing some of the egg mixture on the tortilla and then adding whatever other ingredients they desire.

8. A word of caution: Give each member of the group a plate and fork. More often than not imaginative "builders" will wind up with a tortilla so filled with ingredients that it can't be lifted whole from the plate.

(You can allow the diners even more choice by putting the sausage and mushrooms on separate plates.)

We also make some traditional breakfasts that might include fried breakfast sausages and pancakes or bacon and eggs with toast. The toast can be prepared over the cooking grates on the least hot edge of the fire.

Trail Breakfast

1. Start by frying and then reserving bacon that has been cut into small pieces.

2. Put chopped onions, chopped green pepper, and maybe a little chopped garlic into the pan containing some of the bacon grease or vegetable oil. Sauté.

3. Add mushrooms and sauté.

4. Beat the required number of eggs and pour into the pan along with the bacon.

5. Scramble the whole mixture to the desired degree of doneness. As with the eggs in a nest, it is a complete breakfast from a single pan.

Herbed Chicken

1. Use chicken that has been cut into pieces — drumsticks, thighs, wings, breast.

2. Brown the chicken on the grill. This is sometimes easier said than done. If the fire is quite hot, the chicken fat will drip onto the coals, and flames will sprout up. For this phase of the preparation,

keep the heat-resistant gloves on and a long fork ready. Move or remove the chicken as needed so that it doesn't burn.

3. Line the cooking vessel with uncooked bacon to provide flavor and to prevent ingredients from sticking to the bottom.

4. Place browned chicken on top of the bacon. Then fill the pan with peeled, sliced potatoes; sliced carrots; sliced onions; and some cloves of sliced garlic and other cloves of garlic still in the husk.

5. Season the whole dish rather generously with dried basil, a bit of thyme, a fairly generous amount of rosemary, garlic pepper, and a dash of garlic salt.

6. Add about one-quarter of a cup of water. Place the lid tightly on the pan and set it over hot coals.

This is one dish that you do not want to check on repeatedly. Every time the cover is lifted, you lose the steam facilitating the cooking. Leave it at least forty-five minutes before checking the first time. Normally, when the carrots reach a firm but tender stage, the whole dish will be ready. Total cooking time should take about one hour.

It is a tasty meal, and, again, only one cooking vessel is involved.

Caesar Tenderloin

Ron Sailer, a friend from Kentucky, gets the credit for the following marinade for pork tenderloin.

1. Place Caesar salad dressing into a sealable plastic bag and add the pork tenderloins. Marinate as long as is practical. If you are in camp and can keep the tenderloins cool, marinate them all day.

2. When the coals are glowing red, remove tenderloins from the marinade and place them on the grill.

3. Cook to the desired degree of doneness and serve with a flavored rice dish from a package. Another good side dish is cooked pasta with rehydrated sun-dried tomatoes.

The good thing about pork tenderloin is the shape. For those who want their pork well-done, serve them the smaller tail pieces, which will cook through quickly. For those who don't want it overdone, serve the thicker forward pieces.

Another tasty marinade for pork tenderloin is soy sauce and crushed garlic.

Italian Spaghetti with Sausage

1. Sauté chopped onions and some chopped garlic in olive oil.

2. Add fresh, sliced mushrooms and continue to sauté until everything is tender.

3. Add a generous quantity of dried basil.

4. Pour into the mixture some flavored, stewed tomatoes. For our group it takes three cans, and I pick three types — Italian, Mexican, and something else.

4. Add one small can of tomato paste.

5. Add a couple of tablespoons of white sugar.

6. Stir together and let simmer for an hour or two.

7. When you are happy with the flavor of the sauce, cook the spaghetti in a separate pot. Remember, the higher the altitude, the longer water takes to boil.

8. While the spaghetti is cooking, place sweet Italian sausages on the grill and barbecue. Serve them separately. (If you want a vegetarian meal, omit the sausages.)

9. When everything is done, serve. By serving the sausages separately, the heavy meat eaters can have more, and those who are light meat eaters or non-meat eaters can take only what they want. It works better than cutting the sausages into pieces and mixing them into the sauce.

10. Serve with the best boxed red wine you can pack in. There is always a danger of breakage when packing in bottled wine.

Steak and Potatoes

Of course, you can always serve the traditional meal of steak on the grill, baked potatoes, and vegetables.

Vegetables can be cooked right in the can. Just make sure to remove one end of the can to prevent steam buildup and set them on the grate directly over the coals.

The important thing is to allow plenty of time to get the potatoes baked. Simply wrap them in heavy aluminum foil and scatter them at the edges of a hot fire. They will need to be turned repeatedly to get them tender.

Deep-fried Trout

When we are camping in the mountains, trout is an important part of many of our meals. We love to fish, and we love the flavor of fresh-caught trout.

1. Place flour in a large sealable plastic bag. Season the flour generously with salt and pepper.

2. Heat vegetable oil in the cooking pan. One to two inches of oil in the bottom of the pan works best. Heat until the oil begins to bubble.

3. Place several trout at a time, depending on size, in the flour bag and shake until they are thoroughly coated.

4. Place the trout in the hot oil. We want the trout to be cooked all the way through, but we don't want them overcooked and dry. You will need the heat-resistant gloves and a pair of long tongs to keep from getting spattered with hot grease during cooking. When the skin is crispy — trout have smooth skin and no scales — and the meat flakes easily from the bone, the fish is done.

Poached Trout

1. Place each individual trout on a piece of aluminum foil.

2. Add salt, pepper, and about a teaspoon of unmelted butter.

3. Wrap tightly with the foil and place on the grill over hot coals.

4. Turn frequently.

Trout prepared this way have a steamed appearance. The skin will be soft and smooth instead of crispy. It's a good way to prepare them if you are running low on cooking oil.

Grilled Trout

This is our least favorite way of preparing trout, but if you are out of foil and don't have enough cooking oil, it will work just fine.

1. Lubricate the grill just a bit with vegetable oil to prevent the trout from sticking. Don't use much or the oil will ignite when hot.

2. Lay the trout in rows on the grill over hot coals. (You can cover the grill with foil, but you don't get the same "grilled" effect.)

3. The goal here will be to turn them only once with a spatula because as they cook through, they will have a tendency to break apart if handled too much.

4. When they are done, use a spatula to serve them, trying to keep them intact if possible.

A number of dishes go well with trout. One of our favorites is stove-top dressing that comes in a box and can be made quickly and easily with nothing more than the addition of water and a little butter.

Chicken Breast Supreme

This is a fast, simple but elegant meal for that first night in the mountains.

1. Before leaving on the trip, prepare the sauce described above for spaghetti. If you are going to be leaving in a day or two, put it in a Tupperware container and refrigerate. If it will be several days, freeze in its Tupperware container.

2. Just before leaving on the trip, stop at the grocery and pick up some fresh, deboned, skinless chicken breasts.

3. Also pick up some mild Swiss cheese — the kind that is already thinly sliced and sealed in packages.

4. Place the chicken, cheese, and sauce at the top of the refrigerator pack. You want it to stay cold but not to be frozen.

5. When you are ready to prepare that first meal at the first camping spot, sauté the chicken breasts, seasoned with just a little salt and pepper, in a pan with olive oil. At the same time heat the sauce in another pan.

6. When the chicken breasts are done — juices run clear, but the meat isn't dry — cover each one with a slice of Swiss cheese. Cover the pan and replace over heat until the cheese begins to melt and turns creamy but isn't running all over the pan.

7. Place each cheese-covered chicken breast on a plate and smother it in the hot red sauce. It can be served with pasta, but if you don't want to take the time to boil water and cook the pasta, just serve it with French bread that you picked up when buying the chicken breasts and cheese.

8. If you have time and want to add an additional elegant touch, sauté some fresh mushrooms. Put them on top of the cheese-covered chicken breasts before smothering with sauce.

Chicken Reuben

1. Gently cook the chicken breasts on the grill. Don't overcook.

2. Cover the bottom of the cooking pan with canned sauerkraut.

3. Place the chicken breasts on top of the kraut.

4. Cover each chicken breast with a slice of mild Swiss cheese.

5. Top it all with a fairly generous helping of Thousand Island dressing.

6. Cover the pan and cook over hot coals until the sauerkraut is warmed through and the cheese begins to melt.

Ham and Scalloped Potatoes

Canned ham can also be used to create a delicious and fast meal.

1. Cut the canned ham into slices and gently cook them on the grill over hot coals. You don't have to worry about doneness as the ham is pre-cooked.

2. While this is going on, prepare a box of scalloped potatoes.

3. When the potatoes are done, serve with a slice of ham.

4. If the meal is to be prepared in a hurry, merely cut the ham into small chunks and stir it into the scalloped potatoes.

We also try to serve salads at meals in the early stages of the trek, but if it is a trip of a week or more, the lettuce will soon wilt.

Rob's Potatoes

Here's a favorite dish of hunting companion Rob Post, who makes it better than anyone else.

1. Peel the desired number of potatoes and pare them into thin slices.

2. Do the same with the desired number of onions.

3. Melt enough Crisco shortening in the cooking pan to cover up to one inch of the bottom. You might try substituting vegetable oil, but with Rob it's Crisco or nothing.

4. Toss in the sliced potatoes and onions. Season with seasoning salt and pepper to taste. Cover with a tight lid and place on a grill over hot coals.

5. Cook, stirring frequently, until the potatoes are still just a tad firm but at the peak of flavor. It is the combination of frying and steaming the potatoes and onions that imparts a unique flavor.

21

SOME WINTER TLC

Most trail riders need little motivation to take good care of their horses during the riding season. However, when winter rolls around and our prime concern is staying warm and out of the weather, that motivation wanes a bit.

Yet, this is the time the horse deserves and needs our attention the most. He is at the mercy of those he depends on for food, shelter, support, attention, and care.

Perhaps the first thing to be neglected when a horse is turned out for the winter is hoof care. We have all seen horses turned out to pasture in early winter still wearing that last set of shoes the farrier put on for fall's final trail ride. The shoes either pull free or remain on until spring, with the hoof growing longer and longer.

Either outcome is harmful to the entire leg. Though the horse isn't moving at speed and may be in easy-traveling terrain, the abnormally long hoof will produce abnormal strain on ligaments, tendons, and joints. In addition, a loose shoe that is ripped free when hooked on an immovable object may take with it a fair-sized chunk of hoof that will be slow in growing back during the cold-weather months. It can also be the genesis of a hoof crack that can result in lameness when riding time rolls around in the spring, or earlier.

When you deem the trail-riding season over, call the farrier and have the shoes removed. However, that should not be the end of hoof care. True, the hooves do grow at a slower rate in winter than during the summer, but they still grow. Don't just forget about them. Have the hooves trimmed at least every eight weeks during the winter and more frequently if you have a horse whose hoof growth demands it.

Always remember that some lameness problems that develop in the summer trail-riding season begin in the winter as the result of hooves that get too long and break off.

Parasite Control

Winter is also the season when internal and external parasites can take a heavy toll on horses. External parasites normally aren't much of a problem with the healthy, well-fed horse, but they can attack. Parasites vary by climate and geography.

In colder climates horse owners should be alert for lice and mites that attempt to make their homes and breeding factories beneath a thick winter coat. In warmer and wetter climates, rainrot, the product of a bacterial organism, can be a problem. Whatever the case, the important thing is that you do not just turn the horse out and forget about it. At every feeding the horse should receive at least a visual examination to make certain it is remaining robust and healthy, with no external parasites attached to its body.

Never ignore regular deworming. Internal parasites can undermine a horse's health year-round. The horse needs deworming in the winter even more than during the summer.

Healthy Diet

The most important element in a horse's off-season lifestyle is a healthy diet. Horses are foragers, so the staple in any equine diet is hay. Unfortunately, all hay isn't created equal, and some of it is downright dangerous to a horse's health.

Parts of the country are infested with blister beetles, some species of which make their homes in alfalfa fields. Blister beetles produce a secretion that can be painful and irritating to the horse's skin, but that is not the bad news. The bad news is that the secretion contains cantharidin, which when eaten is poisonous to horses.

Often during harvest season, adult blister beetles inhabit alfalfa fields and feed on the plant's foliage and flowering parts. This means that the beetles can wind up inside hay bales. And, because blister beetles tend to congregate, a small number of alfalfa bales may be infested with a great many individual beetles.

Horses that consume two to five blister beetles can get colic, and horses that eat more may die. Even the dried remains of blister beetles in alfalfa hay are toxic to horses.

First cuttings of alfalfa are rarely infested, so feeding hay harvested early in the season, generally speaking, is one way to insure that the beetles aren't present.

Blister beetles appear in varied sections of the country. The best way to determine if they are a concern where you live or where the hay you purchase is grown is to contact the county agricultural extension agent or your veterinarian.

Hay Quality

Quality is a major concern when buying and feeding hay. It is imperative that the hay be free of dust and mold. Both can wreak havoc with a horse's respiratory system, setting the stage for what can be irreversible damage.

This is especially true if the hay is fed in a manger, feed bunk, or bale feeder. Horses love to bury their noses in hay, seeking out the most succulent tidbits. The problem is that they must continue to breathe while doing so, often inhaling damaging dust and mold.

Make sure to feed good hay.

These agents inflame and damage the delicate airways and may ultimately bring on chronic obstructive pulmonary disease, better known as heaves, a condition that inhibits normal respiration. Because of the damage within the intricate airway system, the horse is unable to expel air easily and must use its abdominal muscles to force air out of the lungs.

Needless to say, this can greatly compromise a horse's ability to do anything that requires an increased respiration rate, including trail riding.

Mold also is toxic to horses and, in serious cases, can bring on a case of colic. It has also been implicated in abortions.

So, rule number one is to make certain that your horse's hay is dust and mold free. The second consideration involves nutritive content.

Hay provides the bulk of a horse's nutritional needs, but just how those nutrients are distributed varies in different types of hay. Generally, hays are high in calcium and low in phosphorus while most grains are high in phosphorus and low in calcium. Thus, if a horse's diet is supplemented with grain, the two may balance out.

Hay also contains high levels of potassium and vitamins A, E, K, and D, the latter if the hay is sun-cured as is most hay fed to horses. It is important to note that the younger the hay, the higher the vitamin content. For example, hay that has been baled for a year or more may contain little or no Vitamin A.

Protein

Hay's protein content can vary greatly. Alfalfa, for example, can be 20 percent and higher in crude protein, while timothy, Bermuda grass, and orchard grass will average between 11 percent and 14 percent crude protein and may even drop into the lower single digits. The time of harvest strongly affects protein content. Hay cut early will be high in protein while that cut in mid-bloom and beyond will be much lower.

The question to be considered here is the amount of protein needed. The diet of young, growing horses and lactating mares requires a great deal of protein. Mature horses need much less.

The best approach is to feed a mixture of alfalfa and grass.

How the hay is fed also can be important. If the hay is the least bit dusty, for example, the worst thing you can do is feed it in a manger unless you have soaked the hay in water first. Even then, that method isn't recommended. If you are forced to feed somewhat dusty hay, spread it on the ground outdoors and dampen the hay with water.

A number of horse owners have switched to feeding large, round bales in specially designed feeders. This can be easy and labor saving if you have the equipment to lift and move the heavy bales. However, it is critical that hay fed this way be totally free of dust and mold because horses will inevitably burrow their noses deeply into the bale to find choice morsels.

You also should be aware that round bales stored outside and without covering can develop a moldy outer layer that should be peeled away.

The best way to determine if hay is good quality is to have the nutrient content analyzed in a laboratory. The second-best way is to break open a bale and both look at and sniff the contents. If a cloud of dust erupts, your decision is easy. This hay isn't for your horse. If, however, the interior of the bale is dust-free, is green, has fresh-appearing leaves, and has a pleasant, slightly sweet smell, you are on the right track. This won't tell you the nutritive content, but you can rest assured the hay will not compromise the horse's health. Very likely it also is nutritious.

Quantity of Feed

Horse owners are frequently perplexed by how much to feed and how often. What is adequate for a compact Quarter Horse, for example, may not be enough for a seventeen-hand, rangy Thoroughbred. As a rule of thumb, nutritionists suggest that you feed 1 percent to 2 percent of a horse's body weight in hay each day. Your horse's physical condition will dictate what you do from there.

To determine the number of feedings per day, remember that horses are grazers with small stomachs. If given their choice, horses will

Horses eat small amounts frequently.

eat small amounts frequently. I have fed hay free choice and found that horses consume no more than when I am feeding them a set amount at regular intervals.

Feeding hay free choice also provides another positive. Horses that are busy chewing on hay whenever they choose generally are not horses that will begin chewing on boards, barn walls, or even each other's tails and manes out of boredom.

If horses aren't fed on a free-choice basis, they should be given hay several times a day rather than a large amount at a single feeding. I have always felt that feeding twice a day was the minimum.

Grain in Diet

Also to be considered in the winter-care program is whether grain should be fed as a supplement or whether hay alone is sufficient. I have gone both ways. When I have good-quality alfalfa or alfalfa-mix hay, I generally let it be the complete diet for our wintering trail horses. (Of course, it should again be noted that horses are individuals. Hay only might be sufficient for most, but if an individual in the group doesn't fare well under that program, feed it grain as well.)

When the hay quality has not been high, we have supplemented with grain. Still one of the most popular and safe grains is oats. It is about 11 percent to 12 percent crude protein, so it makes a good supplement if you are feeding a legume hay that is high in protein. The way oats' kernels are constructed makes them easy eating for horses unless the animals are very young, very old, or have tooth problems. The hull is relatively soft and can be easily crushed between a horse's teeth. Since oats are less vulnerable to molds than most other grains, they are a safe part of a horse's diet.

Perhaps the next most popular grain for horses is corn, a very dense feed low in fiber and high in starch. It is even lower than oats in crude protein content, generally running from about 8 percent to 10 percent. Because of its weight and density, you would not substitute the same quantity of corn for oats in a horse's diet. A little corn goes a long way.

Some old-time horsemen used to think corn was excellent feed in winter because it produced "heat." This is a myth. Actually the greatest amount of a horse's internal heat is generated by the fermentation that goes on when digesting fiber, such as that found in hay, rather than starch, such as that found in corn. If you want to increase the horse's internal heat, feed more hay.

However, corn does provide a lot of energy per pound and can be an excellent cold-weather feed. Its shortcomings are that it is more prone to mold than oats and is often overfed because horsemen are notoriously poor at measuring anything by weight. The important thing is to feed grain by weight, not by coffee can. Rations should be weighed so you know exactly how much you are feeding.

As with hay, it is best to feed a small amount of grain often rather than one large feeding per day.

Keeping a close watch on your trail horses during the winter will let you know when to increase and decrease hay and grain in the diet.

Winter Water and Shelter

One thing that is easy to overlook in our winter care of horses is water. After all, they can eat snow, can't they? The answer is both yes and no. Yes, they can eat snow, but, no, they really can't get enough liquid into their systems that way. The best solution is a tank with a heater or an automatic watering unit with a heating element so that fresh water is available at all times.

Finally, we come to the matter of shelter. During cold weather months some trail horses are ensconced in warm barns while others roam huge pastures with only a gully or small clump of trees to break the wind. Perhaps you should think of something in between for your trail horses, such as a three-sided run-in shed.

Good Ventilation

Of course, nothing is wrong with a nice, warm stable for the wintering trail horse. However, it is imperative that the stable be well ventilated. Moisture buildup in a barn can bring on respiratory ailments and exaggerate any problems you might be having with dusty hay.

Run-in sheds are a good option.

When we first constructed our indoor training arena in Minnesota, we thought it would be perfect in cold winter weather. We had cupolas on the top for ventilation and huge doors on either end that could be opened for welcome breezes during hot summer days and closed during inclement weather. However, the arena was neither insulated nor heated.

We soon discovered that the cupolas did not provide adequate ventilation during cold weather. In the matter of only a few hours after the big doors were closed, moisture would form on the ceiling. We learned that in warm weather and cold, partially opening the large doors on either end was much healthier for the horses.

In winter, horses are equipped with long, thick coats that can keep them warm outdoors even in sub-zero weather. The enemies of their winter comfort are rain or snow combined with wind. Under these conditions the hair is no longer fluffed and able to insulate. The result is a thoroughly chilled horse.

One of the best solutions in inclement weather is for the horse to have access to a three-sided shed. If the enclosed sides are to the north, east, and west, the horse will benefit not only from wind protection, but also from the sun's warmth via the open southern exposure. And, of course, it is a place to take shelter during a rain or snowstorm.

Your trail horses don't need to be babied during the winter months, but you must take a common-sense approach to their comfort and well-being. Not only is that appropriate from a humanitarian point of view, but it also insures their good health for the riding season ahead.

Index

Photo Credits

Chapter 1: Mary Sue Kunz, 9; Les Sellnow, 11; American Morgan Horse Association, 14; Anne M. Eberhardt, 18; American Saddlebred Horse Association, 20; American Paint Horse Association, 26.

Chapter 2: Kathy and Rick Swan, 32, 33, 37; Becky Tescher, 35; Linda Sellnow, 39.

Chapter 3: Anne M. Eberhardt, 44; Kathy and Rick Swan, 45; Linda Sellnow, 46, 48.

Chapter 4: Linda Sellnow, 53, 58, 60; Kathy and Rick Swan, 55, 56, 59, 61, 62, 64; Anne M. Eberhardt, 57.

Chapter 5: Anne M. Eberhardt, 67, 68, 71; Robin Peterson, 73; Les Sellnow, 76, 78.

Chapter 6: Anne M. Eberhardt, 82; Kathy and Rick Swan, 84, 85, 89, 90, 91, 93, 95; Linda Sellnow, 87.

Chapter 7: Kathy and Rick Swan, 97, 98, 100, 101; Linda Sellnow, 102, 103.

Chapter 8: Les Sellnow, 105; Kathy and Rick Swan, 106, 108, 109, 112, 113; *The Horse* magazine, 108; Linda Sellnow, 110.

Chapter 9: Courtesy of Louise Riedell, 117, 124; Kathy and Rick Swan, 121, 123; Linda Sellnow, 122.

Chapter 10: Linda Sellnow, 126; Sharon Warwick, 128, 129; Kathy and Rick Swan, 133.

Chapter 11: *The Horse* magazine, 136, 139, 144; Kathy and Rick Swan, 141.

Chapter 12: Kathy and Rick Swan, 149, 150, 152, 153, 156; Les Sellnow, 151.

Chapter 13: Anne M. Eberhardt, 159; 163; Kathy and Rick Swan, 160, 164; Linda Sellnow, 167.

Chapter 14: Kathy and Rick Swan, 173, 175, 176, 178, 180; Les Sellnow, 174; Anne M. Eberhardt, 181.

Chapter 15: Linda Sellnow, 184, 188; Kathy and Rick Swan, 186.

Chapter 16: Les Sellnow, 192; Kathy and Rick Swan, 194; Anne M. Eberhardt, 196, 197.

Chapter 17: Linda Sellnow, 205, 207; Kathy and Rick Swan, 206, 209; Les Sellnow, 211.

Chapter 18: Kathy and Rick Swan, 214, 215, 217, 221; Linda Sellnow, 220, 224.

Chapter 19: Linda Sellnow, 226, 231, 234, 236; Kathy and Rick Swan, 229.

Chapter 20: Kathy and Rick Swan, 238, 239; Linda Sellnow, 240.

Chapter 21: Anne M. Eberhardt, 253; Les Sellnow, 256, 258.

Cover photo: Kathy and Rick Swan

Author photo: Kathy and Rick Swan

About the Author

L es Sellnow has been a lifelong journalist and horseman. He has competed in a variety of equine disciplines, ranging from combined training to cutting and from endurance racing to western and English pleasure.

Earlier in his career Sellnow owned and operated a training stable in Minnesota, with emphasis on preparing young horses for riding and driving careers. As a journalist he spent twenty-two years with the *Brainerd* (Minnesota) *Daily Dispatch*, rising from reporter to editor, winning state and national writing awards along the way.

In 1984 he and his wife, Linda, moved from Minnesota to Kentucky, where he served as editor of *National Show Horse* magazine and was a free-lance writer for *The Blood-Horse* magazine. In 1994 the Sellnows moved to a ranch in the Wind River Valley near Riverton, Wyoming.

Sellnow is a regular contributor to *The Horse: Your Guide to Equine Health Care* magazine and has written fiction and non-fiction books, including *The Journey of the Western Horse*, *Understanding Equine Lameness*, and *Understanding the Young Horse*, all published by Eclipse Press.

Other Titles from Eclipse Press

The Agua Caliente Story
American Classic Pedigrees
At the Wire *Horse Racing's Greatest Moments*
Baffert *Dirt Road to the Derby*
The Blood-Horse **Authoritative Guide to Auctions**
The Calumet Collection *A History of the Calumet Trophies*
Care & Management of Horses
Country Life Diary *(revised edition)*
Crown Jewels of Thoroughbred Racing
Dynasties *Great Thoroughbred Stallions*
The Equid Ethogram *A Practical Field Guide to Horse Behavior*
Etched in Stone
Feeling Dressage
Four Seasons of Racing
Graveyard of Champions *Saratoga's Fallen Favorites*
Great Horse Racing Mysteries
Handicapping for Bettor or Worse
Hoofprints in the Sand *Wild Horses of the Atlantic Coast*
Horse Racing's Holy Grail *The Epic Quest for the Kentucky Derby*
Investing in Thoroughbreds *Strategies for Success*
I Rode the Red Horse *Secretariat's Belmont Race*
The Journey of the Western Horse
Kentucky Derby Glasses Price Guide
Legacies of the Turf *A Century of Great Thoroughbred Breeders (Vol. 1)*
Lightning in a Jar *Catching Racing Fever*
Matriarchs *Great Mares of the 20th Century*
New Thoroughbred Owners Handbook
Old Friends *Visits with My Favorite Thoroughbreds*
Olympic Equestrian
Own a Racehorse Without Spending a Fortune *Partnering in the Sport of Kings*
Racing to the Table *A Culinary Tour of Sporting America*
Rascals and Racehorses *A Sporting Man's Life*
Ride of Their Lives *The Triumphs and Turmoils of Today's Top Jockeys*
Ringers & Rascals *The True Story of Racing's Greatest Con Artists*
Royal Blood
The Seabiscuit Story *From the Pages of The Blood-Horse Magazine*
Smart Horse *Understanding the Science of Natural Horsemanship*
Thoroughbred Champions *Top 100 Racehorses of the 20th Century*
Trick Training Your Horse to Success
Women in Racing *In Their Own Words*
Women of the Year *Ten Fillies Who Achieved Horse Racing's Highest Honor*

THOROUGHBRED Legends® SERIES

Affirmed and Alydar • Citation • Damascus • Dr. Fager • Exterminator • Forego • Genuine Risk • Go for Wand • John Henry • Kelso Man o' War • Nashua • Native Dancer • Personal Ensign • Round Table Ruffian • Seattle Slew • Secretariat • Spectacular Bid • Sunday Silence Swaps • War Admiral